T. McGarva

CHRYSANTHEMUM
GROWING

Chrysanthemum Growing

H. G. WITHAM FOGG

THE GARDEN BOOK CLUB
121 CHARING CROSS ROAD
LONDON W.C.2

First published 1962

© *H. G. Witham Fogg, 1962*

Printed in Great Britain by
Butler and Tanner Ltd
London and Frome

Contents

PREFACE   9

1 INTRODUCING THE CHRYSANTHEMUM   11

2 SITES, SOILS AND FERTILISERS   17

3 COMPOSTS FOR CHRYSANTHEMUMS   23

4 PROPAGATION BY CUTTINGS   27

5 PROPAGATION FROM SEED AND DIVISION   38

6 POTTING PROCEDURE   42

7 PACKING AND MARKETING   50

8 FEEDING THE PLANTS   55

9 RING CULTURE   60

10 EARLY FLOWERING CHRYSANTHEMUMS   65

11 BAGGING EARLY FLOWERING VARIETIES   77

12 GARDEN POMPON AND SPRAY VARIETIES   80

13 KOREANS AND RUBELLUMS   86

14 SINGLES AND ANEMONE-CENTRED VARIETIES   94

15 EXHIBITION MID-SEASON AND LATE FLOWERING DECORATIVE VARIETIES   100

16 CASCADE AND CHARM CHRYSANTHEMUMS   107

17 LIFTING AND HOUSING PLANTS   112

18 GROWING IN POTS   118

19 STOPPING AND TIMING CHRYSANTHEMUMS   123

20 EXHIBITING CHRYSANTHEMUMS   132

21 YEAR ROUND PRODUCTION   143

22 CHRYSANTHEMUMS FOR HOUSE DECORATION   148

23 RAISING NEW CHRYSANTHEMUMS   151

24 LESS COMMON CHRYSANTHEMUMS   156

25 CHRYSANTHEMUM MAXIMUM   163

CONTENTS

26 ANNUAL CHRYSANTHEMUMS   169

27 DISEASES OF THE CHRYSANTHEMUM   172

28 PESTS OF THE CHRYSANTHEMUM   180

    INDEX   189

List of Illustrations

Plate   *Facing page*

1 Early Flowering Chrysanthemums. 'Alex. Colson', 'Harold Park', 'Evelyn Bush', 'Velvet Gown' and 'Westfield Bronze'   32

2 'Beryl Turton', a pink mid-season. 'Primrose Hilda Birch', a dwarf incurved. 'Sylvia Sankers', a crimson exhibition variety   33

3 'Yellow Delaware'. A late flowering variety for pots   33

4 December flowering 'Fred Shoesmith'. White, cream centre   48

5 Single Chrysanthemum 'Alabaster'   48

6 'Orpheus'. A large reflexing bloom of lilac-pink   49

7 'King of the Plumes' Chrysanthemum   49

8 The Loveliness family, Salmon, Lilac, Purple, Golden and White   64

9 Exhibition incurved 'Enid Woolman'. Yellow   65

10 Large Exhibition (Japanese) 'Cossack'. Crimson   65

11 A market pack of 'White Hope Valley'   80

12 'Jack Straw'. Deep yellow. A good year-round variety 80

13 'Dawn Star'. A pure white pompon variety   81

14 'Skyline'. An ivory-white formal pompon   81

15 Spoon Chrysanthemums. For garden or pots   96

16 Chrysanthemum 'White Spider'   97

17 An exhibition display, showing flower arrangement value — 97

18 *Chrysanthemum maximum* 'T. E. Killen' — 112

19 *Chrysanthemum maximum* 'Jenifer Read' — 112

20 *Chrysanthemum maximum* 'Cobham Gold' — 113

21 *Chrysanthemum maximum* 'Melissa' — 113

22 Rayonnante or Spider Chrysanthemums — 128

23 *Chrysanthemum maximum* 'Moonlight' — 129

24 Annual Chrysanthemum, tricolor mixed — 129

25 'Weldmesh', galvanised wire supports in the greenhouse — 144

26 'Weldmesh', wire square supports outdoors — 144

27 Effect of flower distortion virus on 'Annie Curry' — 145

28 Leaf attacked by Chrysanthemum mildew — 145

29 Adult leaf miner seen on Chrysanthemum leaf — 145

30 Typical injury done by leaf miner — 145

Preface

ALTHOUGH it cannot be said that there is any shortage of Chrysanthemum literature, the demand for practical information remains unsatisfied. This indicates that more and more gardeners are conscious of the fact that the lovely Chrysanthemum is easy to grow. The range is so great that one never tires of the flowers, even though they can now be had throughout the year. The annual varieties deserve more attention, and the Korean and Maximum varieties are invaluable as cut flowers.

I am fortunate in having had the opportunity of growing many types of Chrysanthemums both commercially and in my own garden, and this record is intended for the many amateur gardeners who already have a love for the Chrysanthemum, as well as for those who have not yet fallen under its spell.

My thanks are expressed to Messrs. Wells, the specialist growers of Merstham, for permission to reproduce the four colour illustrations and black and white plates Nos. 6, 7, 9, 10 and 11; also to Messrs John Woolman of Shirley, Birmingham, for plate No. 2, and to George Ball Inc. of Chicago, U.S.A., for plates Nos. 3, 4, 5, 12, 13, 14, 15 and 16. I am also indebted to Mr. L. Neel of The Orpington Nurseries, for plate No. 17. Mr. F. G. Read has been very generous in allowing me to use his splendid pictures of *Chrysanthemum Maximum*. Thanks are also due to The Weldmesh Wire Company for illustrations Nos. 25 and 26, and to the Shell-mex Chemical Company for plates Nos. 27–30.

CHAPTER ONE

Introducing the Chrysanthemum

A PART FROM the rose, there are few flowers so well known and highly valued as the chrysanthemum. Mention of the word chrysanthemum almost always turns our thought to the highly developed garden varieties of the Oriental plant that first arrived in Europe well over 150 years ago.

So indispensable has this type of flower become, that it is sometimes difficult to realise that it represents but one species of a large and varied genus.

Few chrysanthemum specialists or even amateur growers give much attention to the white shasta daisy or marguerite, once so much used as a bedding plant. Yet this is a chrysanthemum, which may become more popular with the introduction of the yellow flowered *C. frutescens* or Jamaica Primrose. The plant known for so long as the pyrethrum is correctly *Chrysanthemum coccineum*. Then there are the alpine species and the annuals which make a cheery display during the summer and early autumn, from seed sown in the spring.

None of these 'other kinds' will find any welcome in the National Chrysanthemum Society which is concerned chiefly with the florist's varieties. This does not alter the fact that these less aristocratic flowers are members of the chrysanthemum family, and they are of value.

Although it is commonly believed that the flower was first grown in Japan, it was in China that the plant was first cultivated. Ancient records show that it was mentioned by Confucius about 500 years B.C. While there are indications of the refinement and beauty of the ancient chrysanthemum species, it was as nothing compared with our modern varieties. At first little was done by the Chinese to improve the flower, although they did seem to want to retain it.

The modern cultivated chrysanthemum is now recognised under the name of *C. morifolium*, although its exact ancestors cannot be identified. In view of the centuries that have passed since the first mention of the plant was made, this is hardly surprising. We do know, however, that *C. sinense* and *C. indicum* have played an important part in the development of the flower.

One wonders why the name *indicum* was given since the species in question is a native of China and Japan, but apparently, is not a wild species in India as the name suggests. Both are of bushy habit and have single white and yellow flowers respectively. The foliage of both closely resembles that of the modern cultivated forms.

It was not until about the year A.D. 386 that the chrysanthemum first reached Japan, apparently *via* Korea. Even then it was not widely distributed and it was more than 250 years before the Japanese took real interest in the plants. Then by selection and cross fertilisation with some of the wild Japanese species, the flower soon gained importance.

Further progress was made and just before the end of the eighth century, the chrysanthemum became the national emblem of Japan. The highest honour that could be bestowed upon a citizen was the Order of the Chrysanthemum.

Soon the design of the flower became the official mark on all state documents and it was used as a sign or crest for Imperial purposes.

It is not surprising that the Japanese came to regard their national flower as one to be prized and cultivated with the greatest of care. From illustrations available, it is obvious that this flower of the Japanese of centuries ago bore little resemblance to our modern sorts. Although the stems were fragile looking, it was because they were so wiry that they responded to the training given. Even today, it is evident that the Japanese are expert in any system of training and arranging of flowers.

Chrysanthemum shows or festivals began in Japan about A.D. 900 and continued for fifty years. These annual displays were started by the Emperor Uda, which in itself gave the flower the highest possible standing. No wonder, then, that until recently, one of the best and largest groups of chrysanthemums was known as the Japanese section. Now these varieties are called Large Exhibition varieties.

The first mention of chrysanthemums being grown in Europe was made in 1688 by Bregnius, a native of Holland, who appears to have been both a botanist and a writer.

These plants, however, did not survive, and it was over a century later before the chrysanthemum became established in England. It came to us *via* France where it had been taken by a Frenchman, Captain Louis Pierre Blanchard. Of the varieties he brought from China, one survived.

About 1795, plants of this first variety to succeed in Europe were sent to Kew gardens and became known as 'Old Purple'. The plant was illustrated in the *Botanical Magazine*, a scientific journal which, I believe, can still be seen in the British Museum and R.H.S. libraries.

It was about this time too, that the scientific name of *Chrysanthamem morifolium*, which is now applied to all autumn flowering varieties, was given to the plant.

Soon afterwards, other varieties were brought to England from China. By 1826 more than fifty different varieties were in cultivation, no doubt largely due to the activities of the Horticultural Society. The first European chrysanthemum show was held in Austria in 1831. Groups of enthusiasts were then formed to further the cultivation of this plant in Britain, and in 1846 what was to become the National Chrysanthemum Society was formed at Stoke Newington.

Just before this time there had been several men prominently concerned with the advancement of the flower. Mr. John Salter made a number of crosses and raised improved varieties. Then in 1843, the famous Robert Fortune was sent by the Royal Horticultural Society to China, and among others he sent home the Chusan Daisy, from which have come the modern pompon varieties. Later Fortune visited Japan, from where he sent to Britain a collection of choice varieties. It is these which have helped to make the modern chrysanthemum what it is today.

It was from Robert Fortune's second journey that the first Japanese, now called Large Exhibition varieties, came to us. Previously the named varieties had incurving flowers so that the reflexing types caused quite a stir. In addition the colour range was very much wider.

Other pioneers who deserve mention for their perseverance with the chrysanthemum include Monsieur Simon Delaux of Toulouse and Dr. Walcott of the U.S.A. Besides these, valuable work has been done by specialists in other countries.

The National Chrysanthemum Society was not, however, the first society devoted to the flower, for in 1829 the Norwich and Norfolk Chrysanthemum Society was formed, and shortly afterwards groups or societies were started at Birmingham and Swansea. Now, of course, there are chrysanthemum societies in all parts of the country, and the interest in the growing and showing of this very responsive plant continues to increase.

It is impossible even to estimate the number of named varieties that have been raised. Every year sees the introduction of grand new sorts. These create interest and keep alive enthusiasm, in fact, it seems certain that without these new varieties interest would wane and certainly the attendances at the chrysanthemum shows would gradually lessen.

Even in one's own experience, there have been many varieties which have been widely acclaimed only to disappear after a few years. Is this because the modern varieties are highly bred?

Without in any way decrying the many excellent present day favourites, one wonders how long some of them will last.

The chrysanthemum is yet another example of a simple flower being taken in hand by hybridists and transformed into something altogether superior. As a cut flower, pot plant, greenhouse subject or for growing in a window box, the chrysanthemum is altogether dependable. We may have single, double, incurving, reflexing and other forms of flowers, so that whatever may be one's fancy, the chrysanthemum will not fail to satisfy.

In our enthusiasm for the modern large flowered varieties, we must not overlook the fact that there are quite a number of other valuable species, apart from those already mentioned. Among them are some real gems for the rock garden or as edging subjects for the border, where they will produce colour over a long period. Even if a little difficult to obtain, when established in the right soil and situation, they are most rewarding on account of the wealth of blooms they will give, and yet they have only very simple cultural requirements.

Chrysanthemum alpinum, with its small white flowers, grows only a few inches high and has been well described as the Marguerite of the Alps. *C. arcticum* grows up to 12 inches, forming spreading bushes covered with lilac-pink, single flowers in May and June.

C. argenteum, introduced in 1731, is a most useful species on account of its silvery foliage, and in July it carries broad white flowers on 12 inch stems. *C. azaleanum*, which as its name suggests resembles an azalea, makes a low growing plant, often 2 to 3 feet in diameter, and on account of its habit of growth is sometimes referred to as the cushion chrysanthemum. The semi-double flowers, on stems up to 2 feet, appear during July and August.

Another silver leaved species is *C. cinerariaefolium*, with white flowers of no special beauty.

C. catananche has been in cultivation for over eighty years, and in the spring, its yellow, single flowers with a slight purple ray are freely produced on 4 to 6 inch stems, making it an ideal subject for the well drained rockery. *C. erubescens* is a Chinese species, producing in early autumn, clouds of flesh-pink flowers between 1½ and 2 inches in diameter, with an attractive coloured disc. Growing 2 to 2½ feet high, it thrives in a sunny position at the back of the border.

From Korea has come *C. koreanum*, of which there are now many first class hybrids, not only single flowered but attractive doubles. These all flower well into the autumn and the long lasting blooms, growing on symmetrically shaped plants, are produced in large sprays. Whereas the species itself is rather liable to frost damage, the hybrids, most of which have been introduced by British raisers, are exceptionally hardy and do in fact often resist frost to a greater extent than most hardy border varieties. Propagation is carried out in the early spring, cuttings 3 to 4 inches long being taken in March and inserted in pots or boxes, in the cool house or closed frame, where they will soon root well. The Ox Eye Daisy, *C. leucanthemum*, a native of Britain, carries on erect 2 feet stems during June and July pure white single blooms. This is the species which has been used greatly in perfecting many of the modern *C. maximum* varieties such as Esther Read and Wirral Supreme.

C. macrophyllum is a rare Russian species growing up to 4 feet high, and having creamy-white flowers during July and August. Coming from the Atlas Mountains, *C. mawii* forms neat bushes with silvery-grey, well cut foliage, and is of shrubby growth. The small, bright pink flowers are produced on slender stems 12 to 15 inches long. This species will go on flowering for a very long period if grown on a hot sunny border; in fact, there is hardly a time from May until October when some bloom is not seen on the plant. It cannot, however, be regarded as being really hardy for the open garden.

C. maximum, the so called Shasta Daisy, is a Pyrean plant which has become popular as a market flower, and there are now many first class single and double varieties of great merit.

As we have seen, it seems certain that the modern tight incurved varieties have come from *C. sinense*, while the looser, shaggy sorts are derived from *C. indicum*, which is only half hardy.

The latter species is, strictly speaking, a perennial, but seed sown under glass in the spring, will produce flowers of varying colours within 5 or 6 months from the sowing time.

C. nipponicum, from Japan, grows 10 to 12 inches high and has quite attractive, if small, pink flowers. Another single flowering species, *C. rubellum*, was first introduced under the name of *C. erubescens* and received an Award of Garden Merit from the R.H.S. under the latter name. Careful work by hybridists has resulted in the introduction of many very beautiful single and double varieties of rubellum, all of which are of easy culture and the flowers have an extremely long life.

C. uliginosum, which means 'growing in swamps', has large white, daisy-like flowers during September and October and often grows up to 6 feet high, and is therefore valuable at the back of an herbaceous border.

There are many other species, but these are some which are both useful and likely to be obtainable at the present time.

CHAPTER TWO

Sites, Soils and Fertilisers

WHILE THE chrysanthemum is not difficult to grow, like any other plant it will yield its finest results when the grower is prepared to pay attention to its needs. Of these, soil requirements are vitally important. As far as the outdoor varieties are concerned, some thought must be given to the selection of site and aspect. In many small gardens there will, of course, be no alternative positions available.

Frost pockets should be avoided, for in them the air does not circulate freely. For preference, therefore, choose a site above low lying positions. Not only will this be avoiding frost pockets but there will be less likelihood of fogs, which are harmful to the plants and which, in or near industrial towns or cities, may further spoil the blooms by the atmospheric soot they bring.

Where chrysanthemums are grown on a large scale and are to be used for rotation in mobile and similar glass structures, it will be obvious that a fairly level site should be chosen. This makes it easier when the glass has to be moved.

As far as the early flowering varieties are concerned, these are normally planted outdoors from late April onwards. Well before that time, the soil should be brought into the right condition to allow the plants to produce of their best.

Chrysanthemums cannot be grown really well unless there is plenty of humus in the soil. Organic matter opens up a stiff soil leading to a good root action. In addition, it retains moisture, so essential during the summer for such strong growing, leafy plants.

Farmyard manure is ideal for working into the ground during the winter, but since it can rarely be obtained in sufficient quantities, substitutes have to be used. These include good 'mature' compost or decayed vegetable matter, spent hops, shoddy, sewage sludge composted with straw or peat, and bone meal. All of these should be worked fairly deeply into the soil, for shallow cultivation means quick drying out in summer, preventing really good results.

The soil should not lack lime for chrysanthemums dislike an acid soil, this being a frequent cause of indifferent results. Lime is usually applied after digging or ploughing has been done. Carbonate of lime or ground chalk is the most generally useful form, and the safest. It is the presence or absence of lime that determines whether a soil is acid, neutral or alkaline. The term generally used is pH, of which there are fourteen degrees, pH 7 being neutral; under this figure, soil is acid, over it is alkaline. Therefore, an application of lime must increase the pH content. There are several methods by which it is possible to determine whether soil needs lime, and the necessary material can be supplied by horticultural sundriesmen.

Where lime is necessary, it is applied as a light dressing at $\frac{1}{4}$ ounce to the square yard, which is 10 cwt. per acre, or if a heavy dressing is called for, double this quantity can be given. The optimum pH for chrysanthemums is 6·0.

If the ground has been kept in the right condition, with regular additions of manure or good compost, there is not often any need to resort to dressings of fertilisers. Good ground contains all the trace elements we so often hear about, and it is very rarely that any are absent in well treated land.

Occasionally, in light sandy soil, pale yellow markings appear between the veins on the leaves. They may be due to lack of magnesium, an essential part of chlorophyll, the green pigment of the leaves. This shortage can be made up by applying magnesium sulphate – Epsom Salts – at the rate of a teaspoonful to each plant, and watered in. Such treatment usually brings first class results. It is better, however, to make sure that the ground is in sound condition before the plants are put in.

Care must always be taken when applying nitrogenous fertilisers, for these are liable to increase the number of stems and the quantity of foliage, but too much can result in lush growth and fewer flowers. Here again, a soil in good heart, dressed with real manure should not need any extra nitrogen.

Potash, of course, is necessary if plants are to grow properly. Any shortage of this substance may lead to marginal leaf scorch and generally poor looking plants. If it is decided to add potash, it is best to use sulphate of potash in preference to the muriate form.

Iron is another element of importance, performing an important function in the healthy growth of the plants. Its presence is needed for the good colour of the leaves and for the proper development of the blooms. Iron is nearly always present in reddish or reddish-yellow loams which is why they are favoured by specialist chrysanthemum growers. Occasionally a sickly looking pot plant can be invigorated by watering into the soil a level teaspoonful of iron sulphate. Even with healthy plants, growing in a compost not lacking in lime, this treatment will give better colour to the blooms.

Other trace elements including boron, copper, zinc and sulphur are almost always supplied in the nourishment secured from the soil by the roots.

As a rule, therefore, the amateur chrysanthemum grower will have no need to do anything about supplying them. They will be available in the good soil provided for the plants.

There are, of course, two distinct schools of thought when it comes to the application of fertilisers. Those who support the natural, organic method of feeding, eschew the use of artificial fertilisers. For them, and I include myself, it is far better to bring the ground into the right condition before planting, rather than to depend on fertilisers, which, while often meeting the immediate needs of the plant, do nothing to feed the soil. There is ample evidence that without the addition of bulk to the soil, in the form of manure, compost, leaf-mould, etc., the continued use of non-organic fertilisers leads to thin dusty ground with no 'life' in it.

This does not mean, of course, that top dressings should not be given, for they are often useful and sometimes even essential, if the plants are to give good results. There are, too, various compound fertilisers which are often worked into the soil when the bed is being prepared. These are based on the three most important elements, nitrogen, phosphorus and potassium, these usually being denoted as N.P.K. While as previously indicated, the other essential elements are normally found in sufficient quantities in the soil to meet the needs of the chrysanthemum, N.P.K. are seldom there in the right proportion, unless the ground has been treated well for some years, and the humus or organic content built up.

The absence or severe shortage of one of the three major elements mentioned, will adversely affect the growth of the plants.

This is why the so called complete fertilisers are often used. Then there are the compound fertilisers which are mixtures of two of the three essential elements, or, of course, it is possible to use a straight fertiliser, which is only one of the three. By these means the grower is able to make up for a shortage of any, or all, of the essential fertilisers.

The range of available plant foods and fertilisers is quite wide. Of those in the organic range, which are quite safe to use, the following have been used with great success, both by amateur and professional growers.

BONE MEAL. This supplies up to 25 per cent phosphoric acid and 4 per cent nitrogen. The latter is available quickly, but the real value of bone meal is that it releases its feeding material gradually, and the roots make use of it as required. There is, therefore, no question of applying too much to the detriment of the plants, which can happen with some artificial fertilisers.

DRIED BLOOD. While this does contain small quantities of a number of elements, it is chiefly of value for its nitrogen content. This is usually 10 to 14 per cent, and since it becomes available fairly quickly, it is diluted and used as a liquid feed for plants which do not seem to be making headway. Dried blood often brings beneficial results to plants of which the stems have become hard, and which seem to lack virility.

FISH GUANO. This is fish waste, which is prepared, dried and granulated so that it can be kept for quite long periods without becoming unpleasant. An average analysis shows that it contains up to 10 per cent nitrogen, 9 per cent phosphoric acid and 3 per cent potash. It should be worked into the soil by the early spring, at the rate of 3 to 4 ounces to the square yard.

FISH MANURE OR COMPOUND. This consists of a fairly large proportion of dried fish guano but with the addition of phosphorus and potash, making it, as some believe, a better balanced plant food.

HOOF AND HORN MEAL. This organic fertiliser, rich in nitrogen, is made by grinding up the hooves and horns of cattle. It is not so long lasting in the soil as was once supposed, and it is reckoned that the nitrogen, of which there is about 13 per cent, is used by the plant roots within a couple of months.

WOOD ASHES. Provided they are kept dry before use, this is

another useful natural source of plant food. Up to 10 per cent of potash and 4 per cent of potassium is usually contained in dry wood ashes. These figures, however, will vary according to the type of wood from which the ash has come. Since the potash content is soluble, it can easily be lost if the ashes are left exposed to the weather.

When we come to the inorganic fertilisers, it is difficult to know what to leave out, especially as there are so many proprietary brands, all of which can be of use on occasions.

AMMONIUM SULPHATE. Better known as sulphate of ammonia, this is a by-product from gas works. It contains up to 20 per cent nitrogen, which becomes quickly available to the plants. Since it is caustic, when applying it in liquid form, care must be taken not to let it splash the leaves.

CALCIUM OXIDE. This, of course, is 'lime' which we have already dealt with. There are many forms including Quicklime which, when it has absorbed moisture, becomes known as hydrated lime. It is, however, Carbonate of lime, which is limestone or chalk, ground to a fine powder, that is best for mixing into the chrysanthemum compost.

NITRATE OF SODA OR SODIUM NITRATE. Soluble in water, when the nitrogen content becomes quickly available to plant roots. The normal rate of application is 1 ounce to 2 gallons of water.

SUPERPHOSPHATE OF LIME. This is a good source of supply for phosphoric acid, which soon becomes of use to the roots. In addition, it remains available for quite a long time. It is often raked into the top few inches of soil, where early flowering varieties of chrysanthemums are to be grown, at the rate of 6 to 8 ounces to the square yard.

SULPHATE OF POTASH. A good source of supply of potash, this is quick acting, for it is soluble in water and is not easily washed out of the soil. Since it is not caustic, it will not burn the roots, which is why it is depended upon by many growers when making up their own composts, as well as for applying as liquid feed. Do not use muriate of potash as a substitute.

Although as previously indicated, there are many excellent compound fertilisers on the market, suitably balanced for chrysanthemums, some growers prefer to make up their own. A suitable formula which is often used is:

> 2 parts sulphate of ammonia ⎫
> 4 parts superphosphate ⎬ all by weight.
> 1 part sulphate of potash ⎭

This is applied at the rate of 6 ounces to the square yard or 15 cwt. per acre. If farmyard manure has been worked into the ground previously, the sulphate of ammonia should be omitted.

When the outdoor varieties have finished flowering, they should not be neglected as far as feeding is concerned. It is possible to help them before they are lifted for winter protection in frames or the cold greenhouse.

Having decided which plants to retain for propagation, the flowering stalks should be cut down to within 6 inches of the base. Lightly hoe around the plants, removing weeds and rubbish, and then apply a good balanced liquid fertiliser. This can be of seaweed or one of a general organic nature. Alternatively, a general liquid feed, such as 665, can be used according to directions on the container.

There is no need to doubt whether the work involved, or the expense of this feeding, is worth while. Experience has proved that it definitely is. Results are seen at the next propagating time. Cuttings from the fed plants will be far better than those which were not helped.

If, as is sometimes claimed, liquid fertilisers are more expensive than solid ones, it can be said that properly applied they are more effective. Not only are the quality and quantity of the blooms improved, which brings in better returns, but since liquid feeds are applied at the same time as necessary ordinary watering, the labour of applying the fertiliser is, in reality, cut out.

Whatever feeding is done, the rule should be to apply it little and often. A double dose, far from giving doubly good results, may very well result in harming the plants.

Never apply a liquid or solid fertiliser while the soil is dry. If this is done, the quick intake of fertiliser may very well cause damage to the roots and spoil the appearance of the foliage.

It is no use waiting until the plants show signs of starvation before feeding them. By that time, they will have had such a check as will hinder or even entirely prevent them from ever catching up with plants which have not lacked nourishment.

CHAPTER THREE

Composts for Chrysanthemums

A VERY LARGE number of chrysanthemums are grown in pots. Apart from the fact that the greenhouse does enable some of the large flowering kinds to be grown in pots or boxes, there are many gardeners who like to grow a few plants so that they can be brought intact into the living-room, when they are in flower. In addition, there are some people without a garden who find great pleasure in growing plants in pots.

Whatever plants are being grown in pots or other containers, it is necessary to have some knowledge of compost. In some respects this word is a little misleading for gardeners, who speak of the compost *heap*, meaning the heap to which all plant remains and other organic residue is consigned in order that it may decay and become of real value in enriching the soil.

A potting compost is certainly a mixture, but of known ingredients which, when mixed together for a balanced rooting medium, is able to supply the needs of seedlings or cuttings. It should contain sufficient plant foods so that the chrysanthemums can grow and flower well. It must be open, so that when made firm, air is not excluded.

The John Innes Horticultural Institution has done the gardening world a great service in producing several standard composts. Yet, when one considers the materials suggested for these composts, they are those which have long been employed for growing plants.

While I have very good reason for being grateful for the standard John Innes composts, I do think that sometimes, they are misused. I often have specimens of malformed or diseased plants sent to me, in the hope of the trouble being diagnosed. In the majority of cases, the writers say that 'it must be the fault of the plant or seed, for I used the John Innes compost so that the soil cannot be at fault'. This, of course, is by no means always necessarily the case, for it does depend on the way in which the composts have been made up, and the manner in which they have been kept before use.

Although details of the John Innes compost are so frequently repeated, they are given here to save referring elsewhere when it is decided to make up the mixture for chrysanthemums.

J.I. Potting Compost No. 1 consists of:

> 7 parts by bulk, of fibrous loam,
> 3 parts by bulk, of horticultured peat,
> 2 parts by bulk, of coarse silver sand.

To each bushel of the above mixture, add $\frac{3}{4}$ ounce ground chalk and a quarter of a pound of the John Innes base feed. This is made up of:

> $\frac{1}{8}$ inch grist (13 per cent nitrogen)
> 1 part by weight sulphate of potash (48 per cent pure potash)
> 2 parts by weight superphosphate of lime (18 per cent phosphoric acid)

J.I. Potting Compost No. 2. contains two doses of the standard amount of base and chalk, and the J.I.P. 3, three doses. It should be noted that growth in J.I.P. 2 or 3 is not necessarily improved or accelerated, as compared with J.I.P. 1, but it is prolonged, so that liquid or other feeding need not start so early.

For striking cuttings in boxes or pots, use the No. 1 mixture.

For rooted cuttings in frames or small pots, use the No. 2 mixture.

For plants moved to 6 inch pots, use the No. 3 mixture.

For the final pots, where the plants will flower, use the No. 4 mixture.

Having said all this about the John Innes composts, it must also be stated that for them to be really effective they must be made up from the most suitable ingredients.

Loam must be regarded as the foundation for all mixtures. For all pot work, really good fibrous loam from rotted turf is best. Garden soil is not really suitable, as it is without the remains of the fibrous roots of the old turf. The best loams are said to come from certain areas in Surrey and from Kettering in Northants, but not many of us are able to get this, and I have found loams from other local places quite satisfactory.

Loams vary from light sandy types to the yellow clays, but where possible, one should select one of a medium texture from virgin ground having a clay sub-soil. Turf loam normally contains a good proportion of humus with plenty of grass roots or fibres, making it a little difficult to break apart without exerting some pressure.

It is usually possible to obtain good loam from firms specialising in composts, but where a substantial quantity is needed, it is well worth keeping an eye open for occasions when old turf is being removed to make way for new roads, etc.

Specialist chrysanthemum growers usually stack turf for 6 months or so. This is done by stacking the turves grass side downwards and building up a heap of, say, about 4 feet high. This makes it easier for 'cutting down' when the loam is ready.

It improves the loam if a sprinkling of hydrated lime and a layer of strawy horse manure is placed between alternate layers of turves. If it is noticed that the turves are infested with wire worms, as grassland often is, it is advisable to dust each layer with a wireworm destroyer, such as D.D.T. powder or Aldrin dust.

When the heap is completed, cover it with corrugated iron sheets, or something similar, to give protection from heavy rain, but leave one side open to admit plenty of air.

When the loam is ready for use it can be chopped and riddled as required, according to the stage in cultivation for which it is needed. As far as J.I.P. composts are concerned, the loam used must be sterilised in order to gain full advantage from the proper use of the peat, sand and added fertiliser.

Peat is also of great importance in any compost. Among its values, is its remarkable moisture retentive properties. Once it is really moist it does not readily dry out. It also prevents the compost from settling down and becoming hard, while allowing the firmness that chrysanthemum roots like. In addition, it encourages a good fibrous root system.

There are many grades of peat, their nature depending on the type of vegetation from which they have come. Sedge peats are best for chrysanthemum composts. The finer grades are suitable for the first potting of the young plants, while the coarse types are just right for the final mixture. There is very little nutritional value in peat.

Leaf mould is sometimes used instead. This, too, varies in quality, depending on its age and on the type of leaves from which it was made. It is generally reckoned that decayed beech and oak leaves are the best to add to chrysanthemum composts.

It is quite customary to sterilise leaf mould before use, since some growers believe it may contain weed seeds, pest and disease germs, which, if left, are bound to cause trouble later. There is little real evidence to confirm that leaf mould carries disease. There is no difficulty in making one's own leaf mould. Leaves can be collected and composted, although it takes some years for them to rot down into a really fine, flaky mould.

Sand is the third of the main foundation ingredients for any good compost. Sea shore sand or other fine grades are not suitable. The grade known as 'coarse sharp' sand is required, in order to keep the soil open and free from caking on the surface of the pots. Bedfordshire silver sand is of the best quality, while fine river gravel can be used. A greater proportion of sand is needed where the loam being used is on the clayey side. Washed sharp silver sand is the thing to order when sand is being bought.

Particularly when the J.I.P. composts are not being used, and they are not essential, it is of great help to use some kind of animal manure with the loam, peat and sand.

They are most valuable in promoting vigorous, healthy growth, although care is needed so that only really rotten, broken down, manure is used.

Stable manure is invaluable, not only because it enriches the humus content of the compost, but it is a natural source of plant food. It should not be used fresh, but only after it has been stacked and composted. When it is ready for use, there will be no strong smell of ammonia, and it will have turned to a dark brown colour. Chrysanthemums in pots always do well when rotted manure is added to the compost. Mixed farmyard manure can be used similarly, while both cow and sheep dung can also be used, when they are dried, being particularly useful when it is necessary to use lightish, sandy loams. It is best to avoid pig manure, which is cold and wet and which does not rot down well.

Poultry manure, which has been stacked between layers of soil for a few months, can also be used.

Bone meal, as we have seen, provides feeding material over a long period without ever doing any harm.

Granulated charcoal, up to $\frac{1}{4}$ inch lumps, is another most valuable ingredient to add to composts at any or all stages. Its great value is that of keeping the soil sweet, since it absorbs any poisonous gases in the soil from whatever cause they arise. This ensures that other conditions being right, the root system remains in a healthy, vigorous condition.

CHAPTER FOUR

Propagation by Cuttings

ALTHOUGH the newcomer to chrysanthemum growing will almost certainly begin his first season by buying some good plants from a nursery, in most instances he will want to propagate his own stock in future years. It is, therefore, advisable to get the best possible varieties, whether one intends to grow for exhibition, or just for ordinary garden decoration and cutting purposes.

In this connection, it is better to choose a number of different varieties so that one has a good colour range. If, however, one intends to show the blooms, it will be necessary to order plants which will produce the type and colour of flowers you intend to exhibit.

It pays every time to get plants from a specialist grower who is concerned, not only in making a sale, but in giving good service. He will also be willing to help with the selection of varieties for the purpose the buyer has in mind.

We are very fortunate in Britain, in having so many absolutely reliable trade growers. These are individuals and firms who really know from practical experience which are the most suitable varieties for any given purpose. I have always found, too, that they are willing to give help and advice regarding the after treatment of plants they have sold.

There is one point that the beginner will notice in regard to the young plants he receives from the nurseryman. In a collection of different varieties, the size of the plants will vary. Some will be rather short and stocky, others will be taller and thinner. Some will have fairly large dark green leaves and thickish stems, others will have light foliage and thin stems. This is because different varieties have a varying habit of growth, but as the plants develop they will, under ordinary conditions, all give a good account of themselves.

We do not, of course, want tall, thin, spindly plants and neither does the grower wish to supply us with them. It by no means follows that the sturdiest looking cuttings will produce the best blooms; very often it is just the opposite.

We shall be dealing in detail in a later chapter with the planting and general culture of the plants. Now, we are concerned with propagation. This can be done by various methods, all of which we shall mention in due course.

The main and most simple way to increase stock is by cuttings. These consist of shoots from the rootstock or stools, as they are often termed, or, less frequently, from the stems of the plants which flowered in the previous year. To obtain really satisfactory results, it is advisable, in fact necessary, to inspect the growing plants from time to time so that when they are flowering suitable stock plants can be marked. There is no point in perpetuating any sorts which appear to be unhealthy or inferior, even if one is unable to determine the cause. Always avoid plants which are producing distorted flowers, for it is possible they are affected by virus. Plants suspected of having eelworm should also be discarded unless the warm water treatment, for destroying these pests, can be given. Carelessness in selecting stock plants will result in quick deterioration, and it is rarely worth while propagating from plants showing even minor variations in form of flower or growth.

When the selected plants have finished flowering, they should be cut down to about 6 inches from the ground. This will direct the flow of sap to the lower part of the plant, especially if any remaining fairly large leaves and soft growth are removed. Cutting down must not be delayed, particularly with the varieties which must have an early start, such as the Large Exhibition varieties.

The outdoor stools should be lifted before the ground becomes too wet and not later than the second week in November. Cut off any long roots, after which they can be put into soil in the cool greenhouse or can be placed in boxes, being surrounded by fine soil, and stood in the cold frame. Give them a light sprinkling of water, both to bring the soil in close contact with the roots, and to keep them from shrinking. They will not need much water during the next few months—just enough to keep them from shrivelling.

Many indoor chrysanthemums are grown in pots; these, too,

should be cut down, but keep them standing in full light. If placed under the staging for a period, as they sometimes are, they will throw up weak, thin growths of little use for propagation. Plants growing in the greenhouse border can be given similar treatment, in order to encourage the production of good basal growths for cuttings. Where possible, however, it is more convenient for taking the cuttings if the stools are lifted and stood on the staging or greenhouse bench. It is satisfactory to remove most of the soil. This will save space. Where available, the stools can rest on the normal cinder layer such as is used for pot plants. They can be packed round with compost, such as the John Innes No. 1, or, of course, the stools can be placed in boxes of the same compost. However they are planted, it is important to see that each stool is placed separately, so that there is no possibility of mixing the cuttings when they are being taken. Sufficient compost should be placed over the stools so that they are at least ½ inch deeper than they were in their previous growing positions. This will encourage more and better growths. Here again, it is advisable to give the planted stools a light watering to settle the compost around the roots. Subsequently, only light waterings will be needed, preferably given with a rosed can.

High temperatures are not needed; in fact, they should be

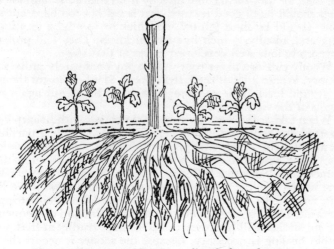

Fig. 1.—The best cuttings come directly from the roots.

avoided, and 50 degrees F. should be regarded as the maximum during the winter and early spring months. One may perhaps be tempted to provide greater warmth with the idea of producing quicker growth and more cuttings. Do not do this, for while it may produce some quicker growth, the shoots are likely to be poor and thin and lack the stamina required for good cuttings.

Fairly recently, some interest has been aroused in regard to the vernalisation treatment of certain varieties of chrysanthemums. This applies to either the stock plants or the rooted cuttings taken from them. The idea is to keep the plants for a few weeks in cold greenhouses where the night temperature does not exceed 40 degrees F.

This is not difficult for growers who do not heat their glass-houses. We need to know much more about this matter before making any definite statements. It does seem as if vernalisation is helpful to some varieties, particularly those sorts which are inclined to produce a rosette of basal leaves, instead of sending up the normal stems. This behaviour appears to be the result of the stock plants being kept in too high a temperature during the winter months.

It is easier to talk about the ideal cutting than it is to produce it. Basal shoots springing from the soil and away from the stems are best, for they have come directly from the roots. Suitable cuttings should be of good texture, that is neither too hard nor soft. They should be short jointed, not thick or woody, 2 to 3 inches long and, ideally, $\frac{1}{8}$ inch in stem thickness. They will probably have up to four well developed leaves at that stage.

Woody cuttings never root well, sappy ones rarely prove satisfactory. Where a lot of the latter appear, it is best to cut them off at ground level. This encourages them to break out again with shoots of the right quality.

When taking the cuttings, remove the shoots with a sharp knife, inserted just beneath the surface, in order to include a portion of blanched stem which will produce the first roots more quickly than if the base of the stem is green. A clean, square cut is made immediately beneath a leaf joint. Remove the lower leaves taking care not to tear the stem when doing so. If the stems are a little soft, cut off the leaves close to the stem, rather than stripping them off. There is greater cell activity at a joint and consequently, the cut surface will heal over or callus more readily at that point. Rapid healing is necessary, because the sooner it occurs the less will be the likelihood of the entry of disease organisms.

Before the cuttings are taken, trays or large pots should be got ready by filling them with John Innes compost No. 1 or something similar. For preference, these should have been made up and stood in the greenhouse, to warm up, for some days. The normal 2½ inch deep seed trays are very suitable and the standard size of 8 by 14 inches will take forty cuttings – five rows of eight. They will be all right there until the first potting is done. Fill

Fig. 2.—Severing a young shoot to make a cutting.

the trays well by pressing the sides and corners. This ensures even distribution of moisture which, of course, encourages rooting. If a little peat or hop manure is placed at the bottom it will help to hold moisture. After the compost has been lightly pressed down, there should be a space of half an inch between the soil surface and the top of the box. This will allow room for proper watering, preventing the quick drying out of the surface.

Some growers use the dark coloured, slightly acid horticultural grade of vermiculite for rooting cuttings. This is completely sterile and has a high moisture holding capacity without excluding air. It promotes rapid and strong rooting. The cuttings have to be potted up as soon as they are well rooted, since there is no feeding value in the vermiculite.

There is some evidence that roots produced in vermiculite do not take readily to soil mixtures when they are transplanted, which implies that the young plants have to form a new root system after potting. Any trouble in this connection can be avoided by using weak liquid fertiliser instead of water for soaking. It is, of course, necessary to keep the vermiculite saturated by repeated sprinklings of water and then pressed down lightly. If a solution of liquid fertiliser, say ½ pint to 20 gallons of water, is used, there will be no difficulty in getting a really good root system to form, and one which will soon take hold once it is planted in soil.

Many gardeners insert the cuttings in pots. This is quite satisfactory where a large number is not involved. Rooting seems to be helped if the cuttings are inserted close to the sides of the pot. The 3 and 3½ inch size pots are quite suitable for several cuttings. Sometimes the small 'thumb' pots are used for individual cuttings. With these, it is advisable to stand them in shallow boxes, the pots being packed around with moist peat or moss. This prevents the rapid drying out of the small pots.

A thin layer of coarse silver sand should be spread over the surface of the trays or pots, so that when the holes are made, a little sand falls in and will be at the base of the cutting. The holes can be made an inch deep with a little blunt dibber, thick pencil or piece of cane. Make certain that the cutting reaches the bottom of the hole and make it firm by pressing the compost with the fingers. Finally, water each box or pot with a fine rosed can, which will settle the cuttings. Each box should be labelled, for it is not satisfactory to rely on one's memory, and of course, the boxes may have to be moved from time to time. Keeping plants correctly named does much to maintain interest in growing them.

It is not wise to stand the prepared cuttings in water before inserting them in compost. Experience shows that, far from helping root formation, such treatment will probably cause the end of the cutting to decay. It is, however, important to ensure that the compost used for the cuttings is nicely moist. This enables them to 'draw up' a certain amount of moisture to help them over the initial stages of being separated from the parent plant.

Once a callus has formed at the bottom of the cutting, prior to the production of roots, the leaves are likely to flag, since they

1. Early flowering Chrysanthemums

'Alex. Colson'

'Harold Park'   'Evelyn Bush'

'Velvet Gown'   'Westfield Bronze'

2. *Top* 'Beryl Turton'. A pink mid-season

Centre 'Primrose Hilda Birch'. A dwarf incurved

Bottom 'Sylvia Sankers'. A crimson exhibition variety

3. 'Yellow Delaware'. A late flowering variety for pots

cannot then take up moisture from the compost. This is why cuttings often look so poorly just before they become self supporting through their own roots. This, too, is why it is a good plan to give the cuttings overhead sprinklings of water.

Chrysanthemum cuttings will usually root easily without any artificial help. These are days, however, when the use of powders and pills are much used and recommended for both people and plants. Some growers claim that the use of hormone powder preparations promotes a quicker, bigger root system. The method is to dip the ends of the cuttings into the powder (or sometimes a liquid) immediately before insertion. If clean, healthy conditions are provided, and ordinary good care is given, it is not necessary to seek the assistance of these artificial aids.

It is worth remembering that some varieties root much more quickly than others. Temperature certainly has an influence on the time taken for roots to form, and this includes the warmth of the soil as well as of the air.

It is best to keep the boxes of cuttings in a closed glasshouse or frame for the first nine or ten days after they have been taken. This will maintain a high humidity, particularly if the boxes happen to be standing on staging which is over pipes. There they will have valuable bottom heat, especially where a layer of weathered coal ashes is placed over the staging, and the boxes are stood on this. The covering of the boxes with sheets of newspaper both reduces loss of surface moisture and keeps the strong light from the cuttings. The paper should be removed after five days or so, for, left longer, the shading will lead to pale, weak growth.

An even temperature of 50 to 55 degrees F. is ideal with the compost or soil being, say, 5 degrees higher.

As soon as it is obvious that the cuttings have rooted, and this will be seen by their perky appearance, ventilation should be given and the temperature be allowed to drop to 45 to 50 degrees F. This will avoid much top growth without a good root system.

Heated frames are sometimes used. This is normally where there is pipe heating. The soil is more likely to dry out in frames, although this drawback is avoided where soil heating cables are available. Shading will again be necessary. This can be given by using whitewash or fixing up thin hessian on the inside of the glass.

However they have been started, once the cuttings are well rooted, they must gradually be brought into a lower temperature,

C

for rapid thin growth is not wanted. Do not, however, move the young plants suddenly into cooler positions. This applies to the early outdoor flowering varieties as well as to the greenhouse sorts. Sudden changes of temperature can lead to the disfiguration of the leaves. Although in many cases, it will not entirely spoil the plants, it does rather mar their appearance.

It is at this stage of development that we have to give different treatment to the various sections of chrysanthemums, and this we shall describe in due course.

While it is always best to take strong basal cuttings, there are some varieties which are shy in producing them. In such cases, it may be necessary to depend on stem cuttings if a new stock is to be worked up. It is noticeable that after warm water treatment against eelworm, etc., some varieties are very slow in producing new growth from the base. It has been discovered that only particular sorts show this tendency, and as it is well known that a few, including American Beauty and Friendly Rival, frequently do so, it is therefore best not to cut back the old stems of these sorts so severely. This gives more room for the development of stem cuttings, which can usually be taken off with a small heel of old 'wood', once they are an inch or two in length.

It is, of course, easily possible to weaken plants by allowing them to flower excessively. It is not to be expected that they can do this and produce an abundance of good shoots for cuttings. When weak cuttings are taken it will naturally result in plants of poor vigour.

This is why some specialist firms offer cuttings or young plants from rested stock. This indicates that the stools from which the cuttings are taken are those of plants which, for the past season, were allowed to produce just one or two blooms to ensure trueness. The rest of the flower buds are taken off before they have time to develop. This can, of course, also be done with plants in pots where it is intended to work up a good stock of cuttings.

It cannot be emphasised too greatly that only really strong, healthy, true to name plants should be propagated. It is only by this standard that fully satisfactory results will be obtained. Limp, hollow, pithy cuttings should be rejected.

It is impossible to be dogmatic in regard to the time to take cuttings. A lot depends on individual circumstances and, of course, exactly when the basal growths are ready. The following times are those generally accepted as being right, in order to obtain best results. They are also the times recommended by the National Chrysanthemum Society, and as given in the Manual.

November: Varieties to produce large specimen plants.
December and January: Large Exhibition varieties.
January and early February: Exhibition incurved.
Late January and February: Decoratives, large singles and pompons.
Mid-February and March: Early flowering outdoor varieties.
April and early May: Decoratives for dwarf pot plants.

Where a greenhouse is not available, there will, of course, have to be some alteration in these times. Much can be done by using soil heating cables in a frame, and it will not be difficult to obtain information and help from local electricity offices. The two usually employed methods are the use of plastic covered cables, operated at mains pressure, and the use of a transformer and bare galvanised wire. It is also possible to use such warming cables for the propagation of chrysanthemum cuttings on the cold greenhouse bench.

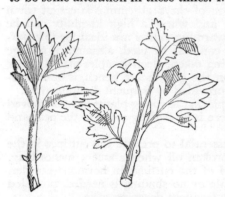

FIG. 3.—Cuttings prepared for insertion.

The summer or late struck cutting method of producing chrysanthemums has gained popularity in this country during the last ten years. It is used chiefly by commercial growers of mid-season and late flowering varieties. It demands the use of a glasshouse during the latter part of the summer and therefore cannot be practised on all nurseries, for the majority of growers have other crops in their houses at that time.

The main advantage of this method is the reduced cost of production by reason of the shorter growing period. It is, however, important to keep the plants growing without a check, although they must not be forced or coddled.

One of the aims must be to keep the stems fairly soft so that they take up water freely.

Cuttings can be secured from two sources. They usually come from old stools which have been wintered in a cold frame, where protection has been given from frost. The lights are usually removed in April, according to weather conditions, and the growths allowed to develop naturally. Often the first shoots become too long before they can be used. They can be pinched back, remembering that about a month is needed before the subsequent laterals will be ready for using as cuttings.

Alternatively, cuttings are taken from the stools at the normal time, early in the year, and bedded out 5 or 6 inches apart in frames. The top and side shoots from these young plants will provide material for the late struck cuttings.

The summer propagation of chrysanthemums is easiest when bottom heat is available, and where a high humidity can be maintained. Electric soil warming cables are ideal for this purpose. A propagating case can also be used, although if a large number of cuttings are being taken, electric cables placed under a bed of sand and peat on the greenhouse bench, is most satisfactory. Humidity can be provided by frequent damping over.

Once rooting has taken place, the young plants must be moved to small size pots, since there is no feeding value in the peat and sand.

It has not been found essential to prepare the cuttings in the usual way; they can be broken off when about 3 inches long. Some growers dip the end of the cuttings in hormone powder, before inserting them. Little or no shading is needed, provided the foliage is kept moist by frequent damping over.

Cuttings can also be rooted in the open or in uncovered frames where there is a fairly rich soil containing plenty of humus. This will produce young plants with a good rooting system by the time they are wanted for planting in the greenhouse border.

Soil blocks can also be used to strike the cuttings before they are moved to open ground beds.

Propagation can be carried out from May to July. One of the important points about late struck chrysanthemums is that since they are planted much closer than the plants raised early in the year, a much larger quantity will be required. The number of blooms obtained from each late struck plant varies from two to five, according to the time the cuttings are taken. To achieve this, the plants are stopped once only, the mid-season varieties towards the end of June, and the lates about the third week in July.

It is possible to estimate closely the number of blooms that can be obtained from a given area, which of course is governed by the spacing of the plants, and the number of blooms allowed on each plant.

Thus, planted a foot apart each way, with five blooms to a plant, forty-five blooms are obtained from a square yard of bed. If three blooms are taken from each plant, the spacing can be nine inches apart, giving forty-eight plants to the square yard. Sometimes one flower only is allowed on each plant with a spacing of 5 inches between the plants. This gives fifty blooms per square yard. Obviously the cuttings struck in May will have longer time to develop, and it is these which carry five blooms each. Those not taken until mid-July are kept to one bloom.

It is noticeable that whereas the terminal buds on early rooted plants are frequently imperfect, those on July struck specimens, are usually sound. This, of course, is because of the better light conditions during mid-summer.

The plants can be supported in the beds, which are usually made 4 feet wide, by wire and string coir netting, or specially made square mesh galvanised wire netting.

The foliage of the plants is usually plentiful and clean and the blooms last well, no doubt because the stems do not harden in summer.

Growing chrysanthemums in this way, does help in a system of greenhouse crop rotation. It is possible to grow these plants after French beans or sweet peas have been cleared, or in warm, sunny districts, the early crop of tomatoes may be finished by mid-July.

CHAPTER FIVE

Propagation from Seed and Division

ALTHOUGH the majority of chrysanthemums are propagated from cuttings and some by division of the stools, it is possible to raise quite good plants from seed. A large number of plants come true to type when grown from seed, which, of course, is why particular subjects can be propagated quickly. This does not apply to chrysanthemums, which, with the exception of a few types, particularly the Korean varieties, do not breed true, hence the need for vegetative propagation.

While some of the first class varieties being grown today have come from mutations, a very large number are the result of hand pollination of certain varieties, having been done by specialist growers. There are several firms in this country that specialise in raising new chrysanthemums from seed.

Since the standard demanded of new varieties is now so high, it means that of many thousands of seedlings raised annually, only a very small proportion are retained for growing on for further trial. Cuttings are taken from the selected seedlings, and at flowering time, a most careful examination is carried out, which results in a further reduction in the number of varieties retained.

It is usually about four years before sufficient stock can be built up for offering to the public. As is mentioned later, new varieties are normally brought before a suitably qualified committee which decides whether the varieties are worthy of an Award of Merit. If such an award is given it does mean that the variety is launched into the world with a good start – through publicity.

Even though the chances of raising a good distinct new chrysanthemum from seed are so small, for those who have the convenience and time, it is a fascinating job.

It is possible to secure seed from our own plants as explained in Chapter 23. Apart from this, chrysanthemum seed is obtainable from most of the leading seedsmen. The raising of the single, Korean, Charm, cascade types will be dealt with when these sections are being considered. Now, we are thinking only of the large flowered double types. Seed of these is available only in mixtures, which are usually certain to contain a very wide colour range.

One of the foremost Japanese seed firms now offers a mixture of formal and informal varieties, including the incurved and 'spider' types. Seed has come from some sorts having flowers as much as 5 inches in diameter. No doubt this particular mixture will soon be available through the British seedsmen.

The best time to sow the seed is early in February, under glass; a temperature of 60 degrees F. being about right. A light, sandy compost should be used in the boxes or pots. This should include peat or leaf mould, which will help to prevent drying out. Since a dry atmosphere must be avoided, a piece of glass placed over the pots will stop evaporation, leading to even growth.

As soon as growth is seen, take off the glass and stand the plants near the side of the greenhouse, since plenty of light is needed. Frosts and draughts must, of course, be excluded.

When the seedlings can be handled easily, they are moved to small pots, again using a well drained, peaty compost. Then, as growth proceeds, the plants are moved to bigger pots, gradually introducing a richer 'chrysanthemum mixture'. The plants will need supporting and tying, and by the time they have reached the 5 inch pots, liquid feeding is advisable. This will be towards the end of April, after which they will need gradual hardening off.

If the plants begin to throw up a lot of basal growth or suckers, some of them should be taken out, leaving only two or three stems. When removing the suckers, take care not to pull off any portion of the small root system. The safest plan is to cut back the unwanted stems to just below soil level.

Sown early enough, chrysanthemum seedlings will flower the same year, when it will be possible to assess their worth.

The colour range in a batch of seedlings is usually very wide and as the flowers begin to open, it always gives the chrysanthemum enthusiast some excitement. It is easy to imagine that seedlings of one's own raising are all first class, but particularly when a fairly large number of plants has been raised, they will have to be severely culled so that only specimens with really good qualities are retained. Even the best of these may not come up to the standard of the present named varieties, but they will always hold a special place in the affections of the raiser.

For the best results some disbudding is necessary as in the case of the ordinary large flowered varieties. If pompons and anemone-centred chrysanthemums are raised from seed, these need not have so many buds removed unless one is wanting really large flowers. It is in the second year, when the selected seed-raised plants have been propagated by cuttings, that a full confirmation of their worth can be established.

It is quite certain that it is unwise to propagate early flowering outdoor chrysanthemums year after year, simply by dividing the old clumps. Not only is this likely to lead to a general deterioration in the stock, but there is the real possibility of disease being carried over from one season to another.

This does not mean that it is never possible to keep and split up plants. It certainly is, and all of us will know of gardens where this has been done for some years. If the plants are being left in position in the border, most of the early flowering sorts will benefit by being covered with a good layer of coarse silver sand or weathered coal ashes, after the old stems have been cut down. Apart from the protection this covering gives, it also helps to keep slugs and snails away.

If bracken or similar material is used, it has to be removed occasionally, to dry off, and it does afford a hiding place for pests.

While, early in the spring, plants from division may look bigger and better than those grown from cuttings, as the season advances the young plants develop quickly, and as a rule they produce finer flowers than the divided roots.

Although I do not think that it is possible, it would be interesting to discover how long one variety could live. The process of taking cuttings or dividing plants does certainly bring fresh stamina, but as far as I know no check has ever been made to find out the length of time a variety can be expected to remain in cultivation.

We all know that many varieties disappear after a few seasons. This may be because they have lost popularity, but often it is on account of deterioration. There are, of course, some old and very hardy varieties to be found in cottage gardens which have been there for very many years. We must remember, however, there were fewer introductions during the earlier part of this century, and it is the continuous flow of new varieties that tends to shorten the life of modern introductions.

Although they are not now very widely grown in this country, some of the Rayonnante varieties are very old. No doubt it is the shape of the petals and of the flower head which gives them special appeal. They are particularly suitable for using in flower arrangements of all kinds.

CHAPTER SIX

Potting Procedure

As soon as it is obvious that the cuttings in the beds or boxes are well rooted, the young plants should be moved to their first pots. They should not be left too long or the roots will become extensive and a greater check will be given, also the plants will become drawn and spindly. In pots, plants can be much more easily fed, watered and generally controlled. It is usual to carry out the potting procedure in three stages, first into 3½ inch pots then into the 6 inch size and finally into the 8½ or 10 inch pots, according to the variety and strength of the plant.

One may reckon that the cuttings will be well rooted within four or five weeks of being inserted into the compost. It is advisable to water the cutting beds or boxes the day before they are potted. This will encourage plenty of soil to adhere to the roots, which in turn will lead to quick establishment in the pots.

Although there are so many different types of pots in use today, I do not think there is anything better, or as good, as the well known porous clay pots, which have been used with success for so long. If they are new, they should be soaked for some hours, otherwise the pots will draw out the moisture from the compost and the plants will suffer. If they are not new, however, they should be washed and dried before use, so that they are quite free from disease germs and dirt. If dirty pots are used, the roots cling to the inside, making for difficulties when repotting is done – and certainly breaking some of the fibrous roots. This also applies to the crocks used in the bottom of the pots; in fact, some growers boil both pots and crocks before use.

Of the substitutes sometimes used, the bitumenised paper pots have proved satisfactory as far as the initial potting is concerned.

It is, of course, usually only a matter of a few weeks between the first and second pottings. One may usually reckon that a healthy plant will fill a 3 inch pot within four or five weeks.

If paper pots are used, I do find it advisable to remove them at planting time, since they rarely decay as rapidly, or as well, as one might wish. This means that if they are left on, the roots may not get 'away' as quickly as they might.

As to the actual potting, although crocks have just been mentioned, by no means all growers use them. Instead they place a little peat or similar fibrous material in the pot before adding the compost. The procedure is the same whether crocks or peat are employed. Even where crocks are used, a little peat or leaf mould placed over them is of help to the roots.

Before describing the actual potting process, we must give a thought to the compost to be used. Nothing elaborate is needed for the first potting, and although the John Innes Potting Compost No. 1 is satisfactory, the following mixture is quite suitable: 2 pecks fibrous loam, 1 peck each of peat and silver sand. Mix these together and then add a 3 inch potful of bone meal, making sure that it is evenly distributed.

When removing the rooted cuttings from their boxes, it is best to use a little hand fork or a wide label, and gently ease the plants in order to loosen the roots without breaking them. Some growers dip the plants into a combined fungicide and insecticide as a safeguard against diseases and pests. Then begin to put the compost into the pots, and when they are about half full make the mixture moderately firm, and place the rooted cuttings on the compost, spreading out the roots and making sure the ends are not bent upwards. Hold the plant in place with the left hand, and with the other one work in more soil, distributing it evenly. Then when the pot is full, gently firm the compost, using the fingers, but not the thumb, which is often used. At this stage, light potting is needed so that the tender roots can easily penetrate.

It is often said that chrysanthemums must be potted firmly. This is true, but it applies to the later moves and not to this first potting. It is when the compost is made very hard at this stage that the roots fail to develop and the young plants become a pale, sickly colour and may even fail to grow at all.

If you think you have potted too firmly, it is well worth re-potting the plants.

Never fill the pot up to the top, but leave about a $\frac{1}{2}$ inch space for watering. This is easily done by giving the base of the filled pot a sharp rap on the bench, which will shake down the compost to the right depth. At this stage, make sure to label the pots, for if not done at once it is very easy to forget, or for mistakes to occur.

After a batch of plants has been potted and stood on the greenhouse bench, they can be given a light sprinkling of water from a can with a fine rose. Do not overdo this; in fact, some growers do not water at all. I do find, however, that so long as the potting soil is nicely moist, a very light overhead spraying of water does prevent flagging. No real watering of the soil will be needed for at least a week after potting. Even then, it must be done with care, for although it may seem a simple job, badly done, it can easily spoil the plants.

The long practised tapping method is still a sound one, for it is easy to be deceived by the condition of the surface soil in the pots. A small wooden mallet is ideal for the purpose, or a tapper can be made by fixing a small block of wood on to the end of a cane stick.

When each pot is tapped it will give either a hollow, ringing sound, which indicates that it is dry and needs water, or a dull sound, meaning that the compost is moist. With a little practice it is very easy to find out if water is required. When it is, fill the space at the top of the pot, which was left for that purpose.

Do not subject the plants to high temperatures, they do best when growth is slow. Depending on the exact time of the first potting, the plants should be kept in the greenhouse for a few weeks, to ensure that the roots are really active. Keep them in full light in a position where they will not become drawn, for sturdy, short-jointed plants are required. It is best to stand the plants on a bench, having a shingle base, and to allow just a little space between each pot. A night temperature of 45 degrees F. is quite sufficient to allow for proper development at this stage, and 55 degrees F. is warm enough during daytime.

Normally, it should be possible to get the first batch of young plants into the unheated frames by early March. Stand them on a firm base of ashes or clinker which will allow free drainage. Should severe frosts threaten when the plants are in the frames, hessian, sacking, bracken, etc., should be placed on the glass. Once the plants are fully hardened, a slight touch of frost will not harm them. If they do show signs of being frosted, and this is usually seen by the drooping leaves, spray the plants with *cold* water, early in the morning before the sun shines on them, and they will soon recover. This is done by nurserymen with great success on all kinds of semi-tender plants.

Do not water plants in frames during frosty periods. They are more likely to suffer from the effects of dampness than from cold. As they begin to grow, the plants must be spaced out, and it may be necessary to alter the position of some plants which have grown extra bushy or tall. It is also a help to turn the plants round from time to time; this prevents them growing 'one way' and also allows light and sunshine to reach all parts of the plants. Ventilation should be given on all fine days so that sturdy growth of good colour develops. Draughts must be avoided at all times.

To determine when the plants are ready for moving to 6 inch pots, it is advisable to knock out a plant or two from the 3½ inch pots to see what the root action is like. If the roots are occupying the bulk of soil and going round the sides of the pots, the plants need moving on. Never allow the roots to become pot-bound, although there is no need to give bigger pots until the plants are ready for them.

I have often been asked why we cannot grow the plants in the final pot right from the beginning, since it would save time and trouble. That may be true, but apart from the waste of space in having very small plants in 10 inch pots, the soil mixture in any large receptacle will soon go sour, if there are no plant roots to penetrate and aerate it.

The second potting, or potting-on, is usually necessary fairly early in April, although, of course, the exact time depends on the condition of the plant, which is often governed by the recent weather conditions. There should, however, be no delay once the plants are ready for moving.

Before knocking out a plant, see that the ball of soil is moist, so that it can be removed without check or damage to the roots. First, have the 5 or 6 inch pots ready, the size used, to some extent, depending on the variety being moved, for some varieties are larger growing than others. The soil mixture for the second move must be richer, and although the John Innes Potting Compost is used with success by many growers, I find it more satisfactory to use the following mixture, which is very similar to that used by some of the foremost chrysanthemum specialists:

3 parts good fibrous loam, not too fine; 1 part granulated peat; 1 part coarse silver sand and ½ part burnt brick dust.

Alternatively, old soot is useful. To each bushel of this mixture add ½ pound of bone flour and ½ pound of a good chrysanthemum fertiliser, mixing it in well. If lime is thought not to be in the loam, ½ pound of this can be included too.

It is best to make up the compost and let it stand in the greenhouse for a few days before use. It may be necessary to give a sprinkling of water, as the mixture is being turned, but it should only be slightly moist when used.

Pots and crocks are prepared in the same way as for the first potting, but planting has to be done very firmly. For this a ramming stick is used. For preference it should be blunt one end and rather tapered at the other. It is easy to make a suitable rammer from an old cut-down broom handle.

Crock the bottom of the new pot, then add a little rough fibre before putting in sufficient compost to bring the ball of soil of the plant being transferred, to about an inch from the top of the pot. Work in more compost, making it level, and firm with the rammer, using the tapering end to firm the compost at the sides of the pot.

Fig. 4.—A rooted cutting ready for potting.

To knock out the plant, grasp the pot in the right hand and turn it upside down. Rap the rim sharply on the staging, making sure not to bruise the plant. Carefully remove the crocks from the base and lightly loosen the roots in the ball of soil.

Needless to say, any weeds in the smaller pot should be removed, with any surface algae. After the plant has been moderately firmed in the new pot, the top of the old ball of soil should be nicely covered, leaving up to an inch space at the top of the pot for watering and liquid feeding.

Care should be taken to ensure each pot has a label, and from this time, too, some light supports will be needed. If these supports are placed on the outside of the ball of roots, they will not damage the fibres.

After potting, place the pots in the frame again, keeping on the lights for a few days to help the plants to recover. As far as possible, do not apply water for a couple of days. If the compost was moist before potting-on was done, this should not be necessary. When water is required, apply it with a fine rosed can to prevent the soil being washed out of the pots and the roots exposed. It is vital to see that each plant has enough water so every one must be treated individually.

Now comes the final potting of the mid-season and late varieties, and it is one which must not be neglected or postponed. It is important that the plants are moved into their final pots while they are still growing vigorously.

In the southern half of Britain, the job is usually started about the second week in May, but in the north, from mid to late May is early enough. We may regard this last potting as the halfway stage in the culture of the chrysanthemum. It is therefore important, since it prepares for the period of greatest growth and the production of the flowers. Neglect or carelessness now will undo all the care given to the plants earlier in the season.

As the time for the final potting approaches, hardening of the plants must be completed, for once they are in pots they will have to withstand whatever weather comes along. This means that the plants must be freed from glass covering by the beginning of May.

All of the plants may not be ready at the same time, and it is important to be guided by the development of the individual specimens rather than by the calendar. Ideally, the roots should be in full possession of the ball of soil without having become starved and pot bound. If they should suffer in this way, the stems will become woody and growth will be irregular.

Properly done, this last move should not give the plant a check, although it is unwise to stop any plant at the same time as moving. Either do it a week before or after the shift.

It is usual, of course, to place one plant in each pot; some commercial growers, however, put in two of the weaker varieties or of those which do not 'break' freely.

If there is reason to believe that the nutrients in the smaller pot are running short, it is quite a good plan to apply a fairly quick acting liquid organic feed, say towards the end of April. Very often it is the supply of nitrogen in the compost which has become exhausted and not phosphates or potash. In such cases, growers apply sulphate of ammonia in solution. Up to $\frac{1}{2}$ ounce is dissolved in a gallon of water, and as a rule there is a rapid improvement in the appearance of the plants. They are then in good fettle at moving time. Generally speaking, however, it is advisable to give a more balanced feed when one considers nourishment to be required. It is little use to apply a slow acting solid fertiliser just before moving time.

Here, perhaps, one should say again that the compost should always be moist before feeding is done. If it is not, there is the probability of waste of the fertiliser or of root burning. The size of pot for the last move will largely depend on the varieties being grown and the way in which they have progressed. The majority of incurves and singles seem to do best in 8 or 8½ inch pots, whereas the others are happiest in the 9 or 10 inch size.

Pots and crocks must be thoroughly clean so as to prevent any carry over of pests or diseases from the previous occupant of the pots. Drainage is particularly necessary at this stage, since the plant will be in the pot for seven months or more. Place a fairly large crock over each hole followed by a layer of smaller pieces. Then put in a layer of fibrous peat, which will prevent the soil washing through and blocking the drainage hole.

Put some compost in the pot and then knock the plant out of the smaller pot and place it on the compost in the bigger receptacle. Arrange it so that the top of the soil ball is 3 or 4 inches from the top of the new pot. While it is best to remove the crocks from the ball of soil, do not do so if the roots are tightly fixed around them. Keep the plant in a central, upright position, and begin to gradually work in the soil over and among the roots. Firm this soil, as it is added, with a rammer. Do this gradually and not when the potting has been completed. This will lead to soil consistency throughout. Bring the firm compost up to 3 inches of the top of the pot and level off. This will leave plenty of room for watering and top dressing, both most necessary for pot plants. Experience has shown that fairly firm potting leads to good flowers with solid petal texture.

The stake can be put in now or left for a week or so. To avoid damage to the roots, it would seem wisest to insert it at once, rather than waiting until later. Place the support just outside the old soil ball and tie the plant loosely to it.

At this stage, the aim should be to encourage the roots to occupy the new soil quickly. This is most likely to happen if care has been taken at every stage of the potting process, and if the soil is in the right condition and is kept right. If the compost is too dry at potting up time, water will be needed early, and the new soil, unoccupied by roots, will be made sodden and may easily become sour. On the other hand, compost which is too wet

December flowering
'red Shoesmith'
'hite, cream centre

5. Single Chrysanthemum
'Alabaster'

6. 'Orpheus'. A large reflexing bloom of lilac-pink

7. Chrysanthemum 'King of the Plumes'

at potting time, will pack down into a hard mass which the roots cannot penetrate.

If the compost is in the right condition and potting properly carried out at all stages, it should be sufficient to give the plants a light overhead sprinkling of water, once they are in their final pots.

After fourteen days the plants will be well settled in their new containers and may then be moved to their summer quarters. From this moment each pot must be treated individually as far as watering is concerned. Always give a soaking as necessary, frequent sprinklings are not satisfactory. Use the tapping method previously described to determine whether or not water is needed.

CHAPTER SEVEN

Packing and Marketing

ONE OF THE most satisfactory periods of the chrysanthemum growers' year, is the time when the flowers can be gathered and marketed. Even if one is not going into marketing in a very big way, there are always outlets for the disposal of flowers. Whether you merely sell a few bunches to acquaintances or are concerned with sending a number of boxes to market, the way in which the blooms are presented can make a lot of difference, both to the keenness of the buyer and the price you will obtain. It is at this period that the grower hopes to be able to sell sufficient flowers to cover the cost of cultural expenses and to have a fair margin of profit.

It is always a great pity and a loss, when carefully grown flowers are subjected to bad treatment at cutting and packing times, for this must result in poor returns.

Anyone who has been to Covent Garden and other markets and seen the way in which some of the consignments arrive will know how important is the question of the quality of the flowers and the way in which they are packed. Treated properly, the chrysanthemum is a good flower for packing, and there should be no question of it deteriorating after a journey of even a day or more.

As far as cutting is concerned, this should be done as early in the day as possible. Many growers like to cut the early flowering sorts while the dew is still on them, believing that this helps the blooms to last longer. On a large scale of course, this is not possible, and many flowers are gathered at other times, although undoubtedly it is best to avoid afternoon cutting should the weather be warm.

Cut with a good long stem and before the flowers are fully

opened, for chrysanthemums will usually continue to grow a little after cutting. This does not mean gathering them when they are undeveloped. The exact condition in which to cut will largely depend on how the flowers are being marketed, and on how close is the marketing place.

It is important to cut the incurving varieties while the centre is still partly undeveloped, for a number of varieties in this section tend to lose some of their petals if left too long.

There is no doubt that if good blooms reach the purchaser, and those which last well, it will mean satisfied customers, and these are needed if chrysanthemum growing is to be profitable.

While many large scale growers prefer to cut the blooms with a sharp knife, secateurs can be quite satisfactory for the job, and in many cases they are easier to use. Care is needed so that the plant is not damaged in any way. It is best not to handle the blooms more than necessary, and if it is a case of taking them some distance to the packing shed, it is best to do so in fairly small lots. Blooms carried in large bunches or in big quantities in the arms are liable to bruise, as is the foliage. Should this happen, the full extent of the bruising is often not seen for a day or so and may be much more obvious when the flowers have been in transit for some hours. To allow more water to be taken up, a sloping cut should be made. Many growers crush the ends of the stems before they are stood in water. This is a further aid to encourage a good water intake.

If the plants were moist at the roots before cutting was done, the flowers, after being stood in fresh clean water for an hour or two, should reach the market in really fresh condition.

Some growers pack the blooms without first standing them in water, although this should not be done during hot weather. They do not look so fresh when the box is opened and this is probably the reason why market salesmen prefer 'watered' flowers. Dry packing means that the retailer has to stand the blooms in water before selling them. This can be inconvenient where room is limited, while there is also the possibility of some of the lower leaves being messy at selling time.

Grading is another important factor in the marketing of best quality produce, and it pays to do it well. It is far better to make first and second quality than to group all flowers together. All damaged and weather marked blooms should be discarded. They only lower the quality of the whole bunch and prove unsatisfactory to the purchaser.

Grading is based on size and condition, and with the large disbudded blooms market salesmen will often say how they wish the packing done. In certain cases the flowers are packed singly.

As far as the supplying of local florists is concerned, it is often possible to grow in accordance with local requirements, and with this type of marketing the florist prefers to deal with a grower who can produce blooms over a long period rather than one who has a lot of flowers for a limited time. This does mean that with established connections the grower can cultivate small quantities of a number of varieties which helps to spread the labour involved.

Packing cases are usually supplied by the salesman and are about 3 feet long, 18 inches wide and 7 inches deep. These will accommodate three rows of blooms at each end, the stems of course, pointing towards the centre. Sometimes a smaller number of stems is packed and, in the case of spray varieties, the actual number of flowers varies. Also cases or trunks of other sizes are frequently used. The grower's aim should be to convince his salesman that the blooms he sends will always be uniformly good.

Before beginning to pack, the boxes should be lined with pale blue, or white waterproof paper. Other colours can be used but should be chosen with care so that they do not clash with the colour of the blooms. Sufficient paper should be provided to allow for the covering of the blooms before the lid is put on.

Cushions of rolled paper are placed in the boxes at intervals to support the necks of the blooms, or the 'cushions' can be made by wrapping straw pads of box length, keeping the paper secure by rubber bands. The job must be carefully done to avoid possible bruising or breaking off of the heads when the flowers are in position.

The blooms should be so fitted into the box, that while they are not crushed, they do not move about. Firm packing will avoid damage to both blooms and foliage. The first row of flowers should be placed so that it is about an inch from the end of the box. As the following rows are added they should be placed so that the 'cushions' on which they rest are hardly seen. When the boxes are packed double ended, as they almost always are, a row should be laid at each end alternately, carefully placing the stalks beneath the flowers in position at the other end. When the full number has been packed, steps must be taken to ensure that the flowers are kept in position. This calls for a central support or cleat, of which the full significance of its use and purpose does not always seem to be fully realised. Sometimes one sees sticks or bamboo canes used – such thin strips will move with any movement of the box, the whole lot easily coming adrift.

It is important that the cleat is the correct length. Ideally it should reach across the centre of the box, so that the ends contact the reinforced portion of the box. A strip of paper should cover the cleat, which will both protect the stems and give a neater appearance. It should be fitted at both ends, to enable it to grip the box when pressed in position over the flower stems.

When packing bunched sprays, no cushions are needed, for the bunches will lie flat on the bottom of the box without bruising the petals. It is always a good plan to find out from the salesman the size of spray bunches he requires; in fact, close contact with the salesman is advisable throughout the marketing period. If it is possible to be present on some occasions when the blooms are about to be sold, it will enable shortcomings to be seen and rectified in the future.

During transit, as well as sometimes in the saleroom, the boxes are not always kept in an horizontal position, which is another good reason for fixing the flowers firmly, and also for not packing the blooms right against the ends of the boxes.

When the box is packed and secure, the lining papers are folded over. If this job is carefully done, this top paper will give a surprising amount of protection to the blooms. The lid should be securely tied in position with either one or two firm ties. Generally speaking, it is not wise to fasten several boxes together, as is sometimes done, as this makes it awkward for moving the boxes about, besides adding considerably to the weight. There is also the greater possibility of the flowers being damaged.

As a rule it is best to keep to one variety in each box unless the salesmen specially ask for mixed boxes. It is also advisable to place an even number of bunches in each box. It is much easier for everyone if it can be seen at a glance that there are two dozen bunches or three dozen blooms in a box, rather than twenty-one bunches and twenty-seven blooms. It is also helpful if another label is put inside the box under the paper lining on top of the flowers. It is also important to clearly label the contents on the *outside* of the box. A stapled card is very satisfactory. This should indicate the name of the variety, the colour and the count, with the grade and the grower's name. Some growers also enter the packer's number. This is not really essential, for proper supervision in the cutting and packing at all stages will preclude the likelihood of poor or careless packing.

The aim of the grower should be to produce and pack produce of consistently high quality, so that the salesman can be sure of what he is handling. The buyer, too, will get to know on whose flowers he can depend, and it is pleasing to both salesman and grower when purchasers have sufficient confidence in certain packs that they regularly ask for them by name or number.

The opposite of this is the grower who is indifferent as to what is packed, or how it is done, and who therefore always has a grievance because of the prices he gets. Often he is the grower who refuses to go and see his produce in the saleroom.

Slightly different treatment is needed with the *Chrysanthemum maximum* varieties. These are normally made up in bunches of twelve stems and are packed single or double ended, according to the length of the stem. Various size boxes are used, which means that the number of bunches in the packs vary in number; this should be clearly marked on the outside.

The blooms are cut while they are fairly young and while the centre of the flower is still undeveloped and probably of a greenish colour. It is best to strip off the lower leaves before standing the stems in water. If left, the foliage is liable to become smelly and nasty to handle.

Make the bunches compact, all the heads being level, and tie the stems fairly high up and in a way that it will not slip. Trim the stem ends off level and make sure that they are dry before packing is done; this will prevent any of the flowers being spoiled in transit.

The annual chrysanthemums are usually packed in dozens and in mixtures, although sometimes varieties such as Golden Glory find a good market when bunched separately. Every precaution against flagging must be taken, and it is important to bunch only straight stems.

Keep the heads level in the bunch and fasten with a good tie, so that the stems remain in place. It is usual to pack double ended in a medium or large box, according to market requirements.

CHAPTER EIGHT

Feeding the Plants

THE FEEDING of plants is a subject on which there are wide differences of opinion and it is something about which one cannot be too dogmatic. Some growers appear to have complete success in using so-called artificials, while others are equally successful when keeping entirely to an organic method of feeding.

The chrysanthemum is a gross feeder and if it is to produce a good crop of blooms it must be treated well. Even so, it is possible to feed too generously.

Although the John Innes composts are very largely depended upon nowadays and there is no doubt that they do provide balanced feeding material, they are not indispensable. Similar mixtures can be made up, in fact, some growers varying the quantities of the different ingredients. Nitrogen, phosphorus and potassium are the three essential elements for plant growth and for convenience are referred to as N.P.K., but there are others. While the latter are usually available in any 'good' soil the three major elements are rarely found in sufficient quantities. Unfortunately, the trend during recent years has been to dose the soil with all kinds of chemical fertilisers, and while in many instances this has meant quick, fairly good results, it has not led to the improvement of the soil itself. By the constant use of artificials, the soil becomes thin and dry. For the development of a proper healthy root system, bulk is needed. This enables the roots to have a free run, and means that the soil is aerated, a condition which is necessary if the roots are to remain active and healthy.

In ordinary good garden soil, which has been supplied with organic matter over the years, one may expect balanced growth. If one of the major elements is in short supply, this will be reflected in the development of the plants. Nitrogen encourages rapid, rather soft growth, which is why it is best used early in the season and not when the flower buds are developing.

Potash promotes sturdy, firm growth, while phosphorus is needed for the production of a really good root system.

If the soil is well prepared and any necessary manure or organic fertiliser is added before planting, very little, if any, extra feeding is required by the early flowering chrysanthemum being grown in the open ground.

With plants in pots it is different, and it really is necessary to help them to support the growth and the large flowers that most of them produce. This, of course, is where the art of feeding comes in. It is not difficult by 'pep' feeding to induce quick growth with a rapid rise in the height of the stems.

There are many proprietary brands of so-called complete fertilisers on the market, but before they are used one should endeavour to discover what they contain. As a safeguard, it is wisest not to use any fertiliser unless there is some indication on the label as to the analysis of the contents. This is often given in N.P.K. order, thus a well known brand shows its analysis as 8 6 5, meaning of course, 8 per cent nitrogen, 6 per cent phosphoric acid and 5 per cent potash.

In addition to these major elements, plants require small, often minute or trace quantities of the following: boron, copper, iron, manganese and molybdenum, iron being needed in the greatest quantity. All of these are conveyed from the soil through the roots to every part of the plant. This is why it is important for the roots never to lack moisture, for it is through the water in the soil that the feeding material is drawn up by the roots.

If crops are regularly taken from the ground and nothing is put back into the soil, then it is not long before it becomes poor and the crop insignificant. If the ground is well cultivated and fed, we need not really worry about the trace elements for they will be there in sufficient quantities. The majority of good fertilisers will also provide the necessary feeding matter for balanced growth although, as already suggested, it is always wise to check the analysis, for it is inadvisable to apply a high nitrogen content fertiliser late in the growing season or when rapid soft growth is already being made.

It is necessary to know something of the sources of various plant foods so that the right ones may be used. As far as organic fertilisers are concerned, apart from the proprietary brands, which are balanced and safe to use, there are a number of separate sources of origin. Bone meal and hoof and horn meal are much recommended for including in composts from the cutting stage onwards. The former has a nitrogen content of 3 to 4 per cent which is quickly available. The 20 to 25 per cent phosphoric acid it contains becomes usable very slowly, which is why the effects of bone meal last for so long.

Hoof and horn meal has as much as 13 per cent nitrogen, which the plant can take up and use within a period of six or seven weeks. Dried blood is often used for liquid feeding, and its nitrogen content, up to 14 per cent, becomes available fairly quickly. Speed of action depends on fineness of grinding.

Wood ash is frequently included in composts and is a good source of supply of potassium. The potash provided is soluble in water, which, of course, is why it is important to keep the wood ashes dry before use.

Weathered soot is sometimes used as a top dressing during growth and it supplies nitrogen fairly rapidly. It should not be applied once the flower buds can be seen. Shoddy is also a source of supply of nitrogen. Slow in action, this material should be dug in when the ground is being prepared for early flowering outdoor chrysanthemums. It is not suitable for adding to potting composts.

Fish manure is of fairly rapid action and supplies nitrogen, phosphorus and potash. Used as a top dressing it is excellent and safe, which means that even if excess quantities are supplied, they can do no harm. It is wasteful to be too generous.

Of the so-called artificial fertilisers, sulphate of ammonia has a 20 per cent nitrogen content and must therefore be used with care. This nitrogen quickly becomes available to the plants. It is caustic when applied in liquid form and must not be splashed on the leaves.

Superphosphate is a cheap source of supply of phosphoric acid which becomes available to the plant more quickly than that from other fertilisers such as bone meal.

Seaweed in its many forms has proved to be ideal for the production of first class, well balanced growth. Maxicrop, for instance, is used for chrysanthemums from the cutting stage and is most economical. The ends of the cuttings can be dipped in a solution of Maxicrop made by using one part of that fertiliser to 400 parts of water. If the compost is soaked in a solution of the same strength before the cuttings are inserted, it brings highly satisfactory results. In addition, more and much better cuttings are obtained if the stools or stock plants are fed with a solution of

1 part Maxicrop to 100 parts of water for four weeks before the cuttings are taken. For outdoor chrysanthemums, the beds should be dressed with Neptune's Bounty 6 to 8 ounces per square yard not less than six or seven weeks before planting out.

It will be obvious that the frequency of feeding for mid-season and late flowering chrysanthemums in pots and the quantity to be applied on each occasion, will vary with the variety and the stage of growth.

No plant should be fed when the soil is dry and growth is at flagging point. If this should happen, not only can the root system be burnt and much harm done but the quick uptake of fertiliser can easily result in the discoloration of the leaf edges and of the soft growing point. Water given the day before feeding will prevent such damage.

During recent years, considerable interest has been created in foliar spraying or more simply put, the feeding of plants through their leaves. This system has proved very effective in dealing with mineral deficiency diseases of various plants and fruit trees.

For very many years gardeners have done all the plant feeding through the roots. Until fairly recently little work has been done in discovering the possible absorption of nutrients through the leaf surface. This perhaps is because it has long been recognised that the foliage has other very important functions to carry out. Although for more than 200 years there have been odd references made as to the leaves being food absorbers, it was not until fifty years ago that any definite experiments were carried out in America. More recently, the use of selective weed killers has shown that leaves can absorb various solutions. It is now generally recognised that entry of nutrients into a plant can take place through the leaf surface as well as through the root system.

Apart from the various general liquid fertilisers, diluted seaweed has given first class results, promoting good, clean, dark green foliage and well coloured petals of firm texture.

One final thing about feeding chrysanthemums. It is not always recognised that these plants have a fairly high requirement of magnesium. Even where slight deficiency may not be apparent in the foliage, the quality of the blooms under these conditions will not be of the finest.

The best way to ensure that plants have ample supplies of magnesium is to feed at regular intervals – say once a month with ordinary magnesium sulphate, that is Epsom Salts. A teaspoonful per plant is about right under normal conditions.

In very hot, dry weather, when a lot of watering is needed and the feeding material in the soil is soon lost, the same quantity can be given at fortnightly intervals.

Magnesium supplies can also be fed through the leaves by spraying on a solution, made by dissolving ½ pound in 2½ gallons of water and adding one of the synthetic spreaders, to ensure that the liquid really does become available to the foliage.

CHAPTER NINE

Ring Culture

DURING THE PAST dozen years or so, quite a lot has been heard about growing plants by the ring culture method. It has been claimed by some that this is a recently devised system. In actual fact, it is a method which has been practised for a long time, although it was not known as ring culture, a term which was, I believe, first used as a result of experiments, at Tilgate Horticultural Research Station.

Whether a small greenhouse or a range of larger houses is being used, the problem of soil deterioration is bound to arise. Since successive crops are taken from the same site, the health of the soil must be maintained, if good results are regularly to be obtained. All too often, it is thought that by giving frequent supplies of fertilisers, we can keep the soil right. Whether under glass or in the open, land needs to contain humus matter which allows a free root run. Thin soil can never grow fully productive plants. It is so often forgotten that roots need air as well as food and moisture. This is why 'bulky' soil produces plants with plenty of active roots.

We must also remember that because of the conditions provided by a greenhouse, growth is more rapid and usually of greater extent than that of outdoor plants. Therefore additional feeding material must be provided. More care is needed in keeping the soil healthy, since being covered by glass there will be no opportunity for frosts and other weather conditions to improve it, as happens with open ground.

It is only fair to say that ring culture, in its modern form, has been used almost exclusively for tomatoes and very successfully too. Some other plants have been grown by this method, including, on a limited scale, chrysanthemums.

Since I am quite frequently asked for information concerning the ring culture of chrysanthemums, it is obviously necessary to deal with the method in this book. Generally speaking, the procedure is the same whether one is growing tomatoes, chrysanthemums or other plants.

Ring culture really depends on the successful action of two separate sets of roots; in fact, the method was, I believe, first known as the two-zone root system, which is exactly what it is. Most, if not all, pot-plant growers, will have observed that at a certain stage the plants will send out strong, and, if left, far reaching roots into the soil, below the base of the pot. It is clear that the first 'zone' of roots are of the smaller type which are chiefly concerned with obtaining feeding matter for the plants. The lower or secondary roots, are more extensive and it is these which absorb moisture.

Bearing these facts in mind, it will be readily seen that if we can provide suitable feeding matter fairly near the stem and moisture lower down, the plants will obtain just what they need and the roots will be kept active, which is essential for the maintenance of healthy growth.

The ring system therefore overcomes the question of growing the plants in the spent soil of the greenhouse 'floor'. It does away with the work involved in digging out the soil and replacing it with fresh outdoor top soil – and even this may not be in an ideal condition.

Some thought must be given to the 'rings' which are to be used. These, of course, are essentially bottomless containers and, as such, must be filled with compost when standing in the positions in which they will be used. This does away with bench potting which is all right for tomatoes, but I am not so certain that it is so satisfactory for chrysanthemums, which really need a firmer compost.

The rings must, therefore, be placed where the plants are to be grown. As to the rings themselves, I believe that in the original experiments at Tilgate, quite large and heavy containers were used. Since that time, however, various types of rings have been successfully employed. These include clay, cement and bitumenised cardboard 'pots'. All of these bottomless containers, and other types, too, have been found quite satisfactory for holding compost and feeding roots and for placing on the 'floor' of a selected medium.

The bottomless pots or rings are stood on a bed of cinders,

clinkers, gravel or sand, which are usually on a tile or similar base. After a few weeks, the roots will have developed and descended to the base of the pots. From this time the floor or aggregate, as it is often known, must be kept saturated. It must remain wet; regular good sprayings of water being applied daily. This will result in the roots soon growing into the base of cinders or whatever has been used. At this stage, too, the compost in the rings must be fed with liquid manure at weekly intervals. No fertiliser is given to the base. It will usually be found that apart from the liquid feeding, the roots in the rings will not need any watering between feeds. This is because the secondary or lower roots supply the needed moisture and the compost does, as necessary, draw up the moisture from below by a kind of capillary action.

As far as tomatoes are concerned, the regular supply of water, at all times, would appear to meet the plants' needs in producing a good crop. Whether the chrysanthemums will respond so well is another matter, and as far as I know ring culture has not been tried out on chrysanthemums on any very large scale.

I am not really convinced that this system is worth while with chrysanthemums. Certainly as far as the early flowering varieties are concerned it is not likely to pay where one is growing for profit for market sales. Apart from the usual labour involved, there is the cost of the rings, compost, aggregate material and laying it down, plus the extra labour for watering and feeding.

This method has, so it seems to me, definite disadvantages as far as the mid-season and late varieties of chrysanthemums are concerned. That is, where they are being grown in pots. The standard practice of both amateur and professional growers is to place the plants (when they are in their final pots) in some suitable place for 3 or 4 months during the summer, until housing time comes round. Whether the standing ground is earth, cinders or even a harder base, there is always a certain amount of rooting through the drainage hole. This means that unless these roots are broken while they are small, they have to be torn away when the pots are moved for housing.

Growers of these later pot varieties usually move or twist the pots occasionally, purposely to prevent these lower roots from developing. Alternatively, they can be stood on a base of slate or something similar to prevent root penetration. Fairly recently, black polythene has also been used. This material, of course, also prevents weak growth, which is a great asset when the pots have to stand on soil of any kind.

Pot plants placed on such bases do not make many, if any, roots through the drainage hole in the pots, which means there is no flagging or wilting, at moving time. It has often been noticed that when such flagging occurs, mildew appears, which is an important reason for keeping the foliage firm.

We must, therefore, consider what is likely to happen if chrysanthemums are grown in the bottomless containers required by the ring culture method.

While we can expect that with the regular feeding and uninterrupted supply of moisture, the plants will be in tiptop condition, the difficulties, or at least problems, begin at housing time. The rings will need to be prised up so that all possible roots in the 'aggregate' are preserved. We may be sure that, as with tomatoes, the lower root system will be both strong and extensive. This will make it a laborious job to lift the plants without damage to the roots. In fact, I think that it is impossible to avoid breaking some of them which will definitely mean a temporary flagging of the foliage, which in turn, can easily lead to the onset of mildew.

Having lifted the plants, there is still the problem of transferring them to their new positions in the greenhouse. These positions must, of course, be made ready in advance, and to continue the ring culture method prepared holes have to be made in the greenhouse floor. This must have the aggregate material of clinker, cinders, sand, etc., so that the lower roots can again work their way into it, and this aggregate is kept continuously moist as was the case when the plants were outdoors, the soil in the rings being given liquid feeding at weekly intervals.

There is another snag we have not yet mentioned. Supposing it is possible to lift the plants from the standing ground without breaking any or many of the roots, how is the plant with these dangling roots to be moved to the glasshouse without some of them being damaged or broken? It would seem very difficult, if not impossible to move each plant individually and not break some roots when setting them in their new places. If they are placed on a trench or in a barrow for transporting, many of the more delicate roots are bound to be crushed and some of the thicker ones broken.

One can only say, therefore, that while there may be interesting possibilities in growing chrysanthemums by the ring culture method, it cannot yet be recommended without reserve. I wonder, too, if there is likely to be trouble from the damping of the petals in view of the necessity of keeping the aggregate constantly moist. There can be no control of water intake which, of course, is connected with the incidence of damping.

Particularly where chrysanthemums are grown in the same greenhouse year after year, as they have to be in many instances where only a small house is available, there is a distinct possibility of the soil becoming disease infected.

Growing chrysanthemums on the ring culture system greatly reduces the necessity for soil sterilisation; indeed, if a really good base or aggregate is laid down there is little likelihood of any unhealthy effects of the greenhouse soil being passed to the plants, since they of course are actually growing in the new compost in the rings, and the lower roots are in the sterile material.

To make this one hundred per cent effective against transmission of soil diseases, it would be necessary to make a 'pan' or impenetrable layer of something like cement which would ensure that there is no contact with the unhealthy soil under the aggregate. Such action, however, would make extra work, since some provision has to be made to ensure that the water does not remain stagnant around the roots, which would then be likely to decay.

As the ring culture method of growing chrysanthemums is tried out by various growers, the advantages and disadvantages will come to light, and in the course of a few years it will be possible to determine whether it is worth while growing chrysanthemums in bottomless rings or pots.

8. The Loveliness family.

Salmon

Lilac

Purple

Golden

White

9. Exhibition incurved 'Enid Woolman'. Yellow

10. Large Exhibition (Japanese) 'Cossack'. Crimson

CHAPTER TEN

Early Flowering Chrysanthemums

THE CHRYSANTHEMUM is a most adaptable plant. It will produce first class flowers in almost every type of soil. It is not
only from the greenhouse that exhibition blooms can be obtained,
for although they will, of course, be earlier than the indoor sorts,
it is quite possible to obtain show blooms from the early flowering
sorts.

No plant will give the finest results unless the soil has been well
prepared in advance of planting. Both light and medium loams
are quite suitable, but it is an advantage if there is plenty of
humus in the soil. Organic matter opens up stiff ground, promotes root action and, above all, retains the moisture so essential
to leafy plants, such as chrysanthemums.

Where farmyard manure is not available, various substitutes
can be used with success. These include good compost which can
incorporate straw, spent hops, shoddy, peat and leaf mould. If
composted with straw, sewage is valuable and fortunately is
becoming more plentiful.

It is advisable to work the bulky organics into the soil fairly
deeply, for shallow cultivation means rapid drying out during the
summer. If this happens, it is impossible to secure a good crop of
blooms. Digging makes a much better job than ploughing, but
when a substantial amount of land has to be moved, it is quite
out of the question to turn it with a spade.

Even when it has been possible to use plenty of manure, some
large scale growers work a dressing of good compound fertiliser
into the top 6 inches of soil. As always, however, it is a mistake to
overfeed the ground with nitrogenous fertilisers. Useful additions
are dustings of bone meal and soot as the ground is turned.

Chrysanthemums resent both very acid, and very alkaline

soils, and wherever possible it is advisable to make a check for lime requirements. There are several easy to use types of apparatus available for this purpose. The ideal pH for outdoor chrysanthemums is from 6 to 6·3.

If there is doubt and it is not convenient to test for lime, it is advisable to play for safety and apply a light dressing of ¼ lb. per square yard or 10 cwt. to the acre of ground lime-stone or hydrated chalk. Do this after the ground has been prepared, leaving it for a week or two before lightly forking it in.

Marginal leaf scorch and generally poor looking plants are usually suffering from lack of potash in the soil. Where, however, it has been possible to manure the ground as suggested, this trouble should not arise. Neither should there be any soft, lush growth, which often comes when nitrogenous fertilisers have been applied too freely.

Early soil preparation is advisable, and heavy ground in particular will greatly benefit from a digging in early winter – then the frosts will break down the soil particles. If, in the spring, it is possible to work in silver sand or clean grit, this will give the finer tilth a more lasting effect. While it is helpful to the plants if the soil is turned over several times, which improves texture and well mixes manures, it should be remembered that chrysanthemums like a settled soil so that the job should be completed well before planting time. Never attempt to walk on, or move the ground when it is wet and sticky.

Since the plants will be moved from the fairly rich soil in pots or boxes, it is usually helpful, as previously advised, to work in a top dressing of a good general organic fertiliser or one of the Growmore types, about three weeks before planting is done, using 4 ounces to the square yard.

The site should be level and well settled, with the top 3 inches of soil made fine before planting is done.

In the Southern parts of the country, planting out can be done safely from the end of April onwards. In the Midlands, from about 10th May, and rather later in Northern districts is about right, but all these dates may have to be varied on account of recent or present weather conditions. The resistance of the plants to cold weather after planting in the open, depends largely on how well they have been hardened off. It will also be a reflection on how they have been fed while in pots or boxes. If, as is sometimes necessary, the plants need some feeding before planting out, a really balanced diet must be given. This should always be light and not over-rich in nitrogen, which tends to produce soft, bush growth susceptible to frost. While still in their pots, plants should, as always, be fed little and often. Sturdy, stocky growth must be the aim, and a help in this connection is to keep the plants, while in their pots, a little on the dry side, without incurring an actual check to growth.

Although a considerable amount of space is saved where the cuttings are boxed, it is at planting out time that the advantage of the pot grown cuttings becomes apparent.

When put into the open ground, pot plants need suffer no root disturbance at all. With the box raised plants, there is always some root damage, and certainly during spells of warm sunshine there is likely to be severe flagging. This calls for frequent watering and overhead damping.

It is an advantage to plant out as early as possible, and if some overhead protection can be given for a short period, this is a help. Here again one has to decide whether it is worth the trouble and expense involved in getting the plants out very early.

In some districts, and particularly where blooms are being grown for profit, it may very well be worth the effort since the necessary light framework can be used again for protecting the later flowering batches of the early varieties.

In some seasons, a late September frost can easily spoil a good crop of blooms, whereas the provision of a covering of light weight hessian will give adequate protection from frosts. All that is needed is a support at each corner of the bed with the hessian stretched over wires above the beds, clearing the blooms by 5 or 6 inches. This hessian should extend 18 inches or so below the level of the blooms, by being fastened to wires stretched each side of the bed. The hessian should be removed when there is no danger of frost.

To return to the protection of the young plants, perhaps a simpler matter is to put in supports at intervals over the bed, and to fix up netting of some kind. On this, can be laid hessian, polythene, paper etc., which will give adequate protection. They are unlikely to be blown away, since frosty nights are usually calm.

Cold winds are capable of doing a lot of damage to early spring planted chrysanthemums, and this is a good reason for not choosing an exposed position. September winds too, are liable to reach gale force, so that if there is a natural or 'made up' windbreak, this is a great advantage. Plenty of light and air is needed, therefore the beds should be out of the shade, either of buildings or hedges. The latter, of course, are likely hiding and breeding places for various pests which is another reason for not planting near them.

Having discussed the soil, hardening off and the protection of early flowering chrysanthemums, we now come to the actual planting out procedure. The earliest rooted cuttings are put outdoors first.

While we need to give the plants sufficient room, there is no need to waste space, since most of us find we have insufficient land for all we would like to grow. Then we must bear in mind that certain varieties require rather more space than others.

It is best to start with a planting plan rather than putting the plants in haphazardly.

Commercial growers usually plant chrysanthemums on the three row bed system for convenience in picking and cultural work. A spacing of 15 inches each way, is satisfactory. Between each three row bed, a pathway of at least 2½ feet is allowed. Alternatively, the plants can be put 14 inches square and a 2 foot path allowed after every fifth row. In the garden the plants can be spaced 18 inches apart with 21 inches between the rows, a path of 2½ feet being allowed after every three or four rows, for cleaning and cutting purposes.

Groups of six or seven plants always look well if 15 to 18 inches are allowed between the plants. Every care should be taken to see that the roots of the plants in the pots or boxes are moist before planting. This should also be so with young plants which have been grown in a frame bed. The latter will have a bigger root system, since they will not have been growing in a restricted space.

Perhaps here we ought to say that due consideration should be given to the actual varieties to be grown, for whereas some are naturally small growing, others make really bushy specimens, needing more room, so that spacing must be decided upon accordingly.

This, too, will help in regard to staking, for some sorts are much taller growing than others. It is advisable to keep the varieties of different heights growing together, for this will present an appearance of tidiness, especially if the supports are placed upright and the rows are made straight.

It is best to insert the supports before the chrysanthemums are put in. Then there is no possibility of the roots being damaged. Bamboo canes or inch square stakes of the appropriate height have long been used with success.

Many of the larger growers of chrysanthemums are changing over to the wire and string framework system, which has the great advantage of rapid installation and allows the support of the plants to be adjusted as growth proceeds. For this, however, it is necessary for each bed to be devoted to one variety so that the height of all the plants is the same.

If this system is relied on, all that is needed at planting time is a 2 foot lightweight cane to secure the plants against wind damage, while they are becoming established.

It is necessary to insert posts up to 2 inches square at each corner of the bed, and to stretch wire both along the length and width of the bed. This makes a number of squares in which the plants grow. The wire 'frame' is raised as the plants grow taller. Full support is thus given with no restriction of growth.

Where plants are being grown for exhibition purposes, it is quite usual to give each plant three or four canes, one for each break. This is much better than linking all the stems together, as is often done for ordinary cut flower purposes. Crowded, crushed foliage, gives encouragement to mildew to set in, as well as leading to discoloration. Whatever method is adopted, staking should be done early and well.

If, owing to bad weather conditions, pot and box plants have to be kept waiting before being planted out, they should be given a feed of a weak organic liquid fertiliser, such as seaweed, at seven day intervals. This will keep the stems from hardening, which would hold back development later.

Pot grown plants should be carefully knocked out, and a trowel used for making the hole in the soil. A stainless steel one is particularly easy to use. If the plant is pressed carefully into the hole towards the soil, there will be no air pocket under it, and the soil is pressed by the trowel. Even a very small space under, or close to, the plant can soon fill with water, leading to harmful results. Complete and close contact between plant and the new soil leads to quick development.

The first raffia or jute fillis tie to the support should be at not more than 2 inches from ground level, other ties being made regularly as growth proceeds. This will ensure that the stems keep growing upright and do not flop about.

For a number of years a large number of chrysanthemum growers have adopted what has commonly been known as the 'stringing' method of supporting early varieties and directly planted varieties under glass. This method has many points to commend it and it has now been generally accepted. Its benefits and disadvantages are known by most growers. With this method there is little rigidity, the whole structure being able to collapse inwards, and the cross strings slip easily, giving too large or too small a mesh. To these disadvantages is added the labour cost of erecting the wires and tying the cross strings, and the wire and string structure cannot be stored and used again successfully the following year.

By using Weldmesh supports the above disadvantages are eliminated and labour costs cut to a minimum.

Weldmesh is made of 13 gauge wiped galvanised wire and is supplied in rolls 30 ft. long by 40 in. wide. The cross wires are spot welded to give 8 inch squares. It can be readily seen that 50 ft., 60 ft., 75 ft., 100 ft. and 150 ft. lengths can be cut from the original roll without waste. All lengths can be re-rolled at the end of the season for easy storage. 6 g. wires of 40 inch length are available as an extra for additional cross and end support, if required.

The following methods of erection and planting have been used and will serve as a guide to growers' requirements. Two posts of either stout timber or angle iron are driven firmly into the ground at each end of the bed in such a way that they are within the area of the outside and end squares of the Weldmesh. A 6 g. rod, a short length of angle iron or steel piping is attached to the Weldmesh on the outside of the posts. To obtain accurate planting distances the mesh is kept at ground level and used as a planting guide. With outside planting it is usually necessary to stake each plant with a short bamboo cane, making one tie only. For this purpose, the inexpensive 2 feet, 3 to 4 lb. length and weight bamboo is recommended. The Weldmesh is lifted with the growth of the plant and is kept approximately 12 inches below the top growth. Any sag in the length of Weldmesh can be prevented by tying bamboo canes to either side of the wire mesh.

Very little, if any, wind damage occurs when Weldmesh supports are used.

Some growers like to leave a little soil depression around each plant. This facilitates watering in the early stages and also helps if later, dry weather sets in and it becomes necessary to water them. Drawn or 'leggy' plants can be placed deeper than the others, although normally there is no other advantage in planting deeply.

At this stage, make sure that each plant or batch of plants is labelled properly. It is unwise to rely on memory. Not only do labels ensure that each variety is known, which increases interest, but they are of real importance when it comes to the stopping of certain sorts.

If the soil is nicely moist there should be no need to water the plants, although an overhead spraying for a week or so will freshen the leaves. This treatment will also encourage the roots to become active in the new soil.

Occasionally birds will attack newly planted chrysanthemums, sometimes they even strip off the leaves. It seems probable that they are after greenfly or other pests on the undersides of the leaves, so that it is important to ensure that the plants are perfectly pest-free before being put outdoors.

Once they become established, the plants almost always produce a number of side shoots or lateral growths. In many cases these side shoots soon make more growth than the main stem. If left, the flower bud on the original growth fails to develop or to open properly. Even when it does produce a bloom, this is of very little or no use. The reason, of course, is that the laterals take nearly all the nourishment obtained by the roots.

As far as the early flowering outdoor varieties are concerned, stopping is a simple job. As a rule only one stopping is necessary. If left unstopped the plants would continue growing taller until they formed a flower bud at the top of the main stem. This is known as the break bud. Usually this stem is stopped, or the centre is nipped out as soon as the plant is established in the open ground; that is, about ten days after planting.

After the removal of the tip of the main stem, young shoots develop in the leaf axils. These are known as first breaks or laterals and it is from these stems that early flowering chrysanthemums are usually allowed to bloom. The centre bud at the end of these breaks is known as the first crown bud. If left untouched, further buds will develop in the leaf axils of these laterals, but in order to secure a bloom of good size from each of the buds at the top of the laterals, all unwanted buds and all young shoots developing in the leaf axils must be removed.

This treatment is known as securing or 'taking' the bud. Occasionally the tops of the lateral growths are taken out which causes them in turn to form further side shoots, and when they are taken the buds on these stems are called second crown buds. As a rule the flowers from these are small but some gardeners think that they are of better colour.

71

For general garden and house decoration, the question of timing does not arise, but where good blooms are needed on special dates the time of pinching out or stopping is very important. The first autumn shows are usually held about the second week in September and this is the period that many growers want to have their best flowers available. If cuttings are taken towards the end of February and the plants are stopped 3 months later, they will usually produce first class blooms in September.

Much depends upon earlier treatment and weather conditions, and while in many cases one may reckon a period of fourteen weeks between stopping and full flower it is impossible to generalise, and the best advice I can give is to consult the list of varieties published by the National Chrysanthemum Society which gives full details of stopping times, in order to secure blooms for show purposes.

Once the buds have been taken, we wait with impatience for the breaking open of the calyx which will reveal the colour. While we wait, however, there are various attentions needed if all is to be well with the plants. Late side shoots must be removed and spraying done if there are the slightest signs of insect pests or of mildew. The breaks or flowering stems must be kept tied to supports to avoid damage by winds.

Particularly in industrial areas where there is much air-borne dust, some kind of protection can be given to the blooms. Sometimes paper bags are used to cover individual flowers, or there are special greaseproof bags treated to make them waterproof too. These are placed over the buds just before they break open. By this method, botrytis spores are prevented from making an entry. While the white and many of the yellow flowering varieties are quite satisfactory under 'bag covering' it cannot be recommended for the richer coloured pinks, reds and bronzes, which lose much of their colour, making them less attractive. In addition, loss of colour is bound to be penalised if the blooms are being exhibited.

A more simple way of giving protection from sun and rain, is to rig up a framework to support some overhead covering. Polythene can be used, although this really needs placing on some underlying support to prevent it sagging in the middle from the weight of rain.

Whatever is used, adequate headroom must be allowed to avoid creating conditions favourable to 'damping'.

Although we have referred in detail to the training, stopping and other attentions needed to obtain first class blooms from the outdoor chrysanthemums, not everyone wishes to go in for this method of cultivation.

Good blooms may still be had, however, when the plants are treated in much the same way as many other hardy plants. Most of us have seen long established clumps of chrysanthemums flowering quite freely year after year, although nothing at all has been done to help them.

The chrysanthemum is a tolerant plant which even when neglected will produce colourful blooms. Just a little care will, however, make all the difference.

Large old clumps can be lifted and divided when they are beginning to grow well in the spring. If smallish pieces or divisions with plenty of roots are put in the ground again, they usually settle down quickly. If once they are in full growth, they are given a few liquid feeds, they will respond with quite good flowers.

While they will never be so strong growing or produce such fine quality blooms as plants raised from cuttings, they will provide colour in the garden and for cutting. What they lack in quality they will, at least partly, make up in quantity.

The early flowering chrysanthemums are plants which can be thoroughly recommended for all decorative purposes and should certainly be in every garden.

It is quite in order to leave early flowering chrysanthemums in the ground throughout the winter, but to preserve the strength of the plants, some at least, should be lifted and protected during rough weather. When October arrives it brings an indefinable sadness to the chrysanthemum grower, for then the last of the Earlies are making their brave, defiant stand against the autumn weather. Slowly their strength begins to wane and they gradually become dormant. To the enthusiast, the sadness of the season is soon changed to determination as he thinks of better things from his plants for the next season.

He knows that if this is to be, his work must begin again at once. The stems of the finished plants must be cut down to within 6 inches of the base and the precious stools labelled, lifted and moved to the cold frame or cold greenhouse. There the positions will already have been prepared, so that the stools can be stood in finely broken up soil which is pressed around the roots.

Only the heartiest stools should be kept, any plants which, although not diseased, but have looked in any way unusual, are best destroyed. Mildew sometimes occurs after the plants have been lifted but a spraying of sulphide of potassium will prevent its development.

A light watering can be given to settle the stools after planting, but subsequently little moisture will be needed until January. Heat is not required until early in the year when a little warmth is helpful in encouraging the shoots to develop in order to obtain cuttings. Meanwhile, the lifting being done and the beds being vacant, the ground can be deeply moved, manured and left rough as the first stage, in preparation for next season. It is best to burn all old leaves and other plant remains and not to turn them in when digging. Once the stools are safely planted under cover, this is not the end for the grower of early flowering chrysanthemums. It is but the harbinger of hope and the promise of fulfilment in the year that lies ahead.

Nowadays there are many people, who, because they live in a flat or may be for other reasons, have no garden but only a paved yard or a verandah. It is good news for flower lovers in these circumstances that the early flowering chrysanthemum can be grown in large pots, tubs or boxes.

The process of propagation is the same as for plants which are to be grown in the open ground, although in the majority of cases it is probable that plants from 3 inch pots will be bought in early May from a nurseryman.

The John Innes Potting Composts are easily obtainable and since it will probably be best to move the plants from the 3 inch to the 5 inch pots, the John Innes Compost No. 2, can be used at that stage. When the plants are moved to their final 8 or 9 inch pots, the John Innes No. 3 or No. 4 will be better, since they contain more feeding matter.

Firm potting is necessary at all stages, and after the ramming stick has been used for the final pots, the compost should be 2 or 3 inches below the rims to allow for top dressing as the season advances. Watering is an important job for pot plants, but provided they do not dry out or are not over-watered, there should be steady development.

When the plants are growing well in the final pots, liquid manure should be applied every ten days or so. This will replace the original feeding material in the compost, which will by then be used. Once the buds have been 'taken', use a feed with a high potash content until the colour shows. Keep an eye open for aphides and other pests so that they can be dealt with before they gain a hold. It will be necessary to make sure that the pots cannot be blown over by gusts of wind but it should not be difficult to anchor them in some way.

There is no reason why well grown pot plants should not produce first class blooms, although perhaps they will require just a little more attention than open ground plants.

EARLY FLOWERING VARIETIES

Early flowering varieties are those which are planted in the garden in May and bloom where they are planted. All varieties listed are suitable for cutting and for garden decoration. Many are excellent for exhibition.

ALFRETON BEAUTY	August – September	Brilliant orange-bronze incurve.
APRICOT SYLVIA RILEY	August	Medium flowered reflexing. Apricot suffused with pink. Large beautifully formed flowers easy to grow and disbud.
BALCOMBE BRILLIANCE	August – September	Bright scarlet crimson, gold reverse.
BRENDA TALBOT	September	Superb habit and perfect carnation-pink flowers make this a winner.
BRIGHTON YELLOW	August	Large reflexing yellow. Most useful under glass.
BRUMAS	September	Semi-curving creamy-white a favourite when pure white is not desired.
ERMINE	August – September	The perfection of its form and the purity of its white make this a flower to be wondered at.
FLORENCE HORWOOD	August	Rose pink gold centre.
FRED YULE	September	Large blooms, rich orange-bronze.
HAROLD PARK	September	Incurving buttercup-yellow.
HOPE VALLEY	September	Pale mauve-pink.
HURRICANE	September	Large incurving magnificent shade of coppery-red of medium height and prolific habit.
IMPERATOR	September	Magnificent deep crimson, dwarf.
JOHN WOOLMAN	September	Outstanding silvery-lilac, incurved perfect flowers, ideal for exhibition. A.M., F.C.C.

KATHLEEN DOWARD	September – October	Very large reflex flowering of apple-blossom pink with deep cream reverse. Outstanding in the garden, beautiful in arrangements.
MARKET ORANGE	August – September	Medium flowered, reflexing orange. Plants are of medium height and the flowers are weatherproof.
PEACH BLOSSOM	August	Peach-pink, large and delightfully informal.
RADAR	August	Golden-amber of good quality.
ROSE WELLS	September	Incurving petals of pure rose. The reverse of the petals is a delicate glistening shell.
SERENUS	September	The best market white for its month.
SWEETHEART	Early August	Rose-pink tinged with gold.
SYLVIA RILEY	August – September	Reflexing carnation-pink.
UNA	September	Large solid incurving bloom, pink with silver reverse.
WESTFIELD BRONZE	August – September	One of the elite, extraordinarily fine blazing burnt-orange and bronze, in superb incurving blooms.
WHITE HOPE	August – September	Large pure flowers of excellent quality suitable for all purposes. One of the best whites in bad weather.
WHITE HOPE VALLEY	September	Pure white, sport from Hope Valley.

CHAPTER ELEVEN

Bagging early flowering Varieties

ALMOST EVERY one who has grown outdoor chrysanthemums with the idea of exhibiting the blooms will know the disappointment of finding some of the flowers being weather marked at cutting time. The covering of individual blooms is something which has been practised by a few growers for quite a long time, particularly by those who happen to live in or near, industrial areas.

Bagging has, however, now become quite an established practice among both amateur and trade growers who exhibit. It is in no way an expensive operation, for ordinary greaseproof paper bags of the 10 inch size are used. It is important that the bags are greaseproof, for they will be exposed to varying weather conditions for three weeks or so and they must be able to withstand whatever comes in the way of sun, rain or winds.

Each flower bud to be protected must be supported with a stake or cane, placed so that the bud is well above the support. There will then be little or no risk of the bag or bloom being damaged by chafing or by contacting other bags. It is advisable to make the buds free from pests before bagging. This can usually be done by using a good insecticide. If one spraying is given a week or so before bagging is done and another the day previous to covering, this should destroy both pests and eggs.

It is important not to cover the buds when they are damp, for if they are moist from either rain, dew or the use of an insecticide, there is every likelihood that the wet buds will heat up and become marked, if not entirely spoiled.

Instead of the spraying the day before the coverings are put on, some growers lightly dust the inside of the bag with Lindane or a similar insecticide dust. This does kill any pests which develop after the bags are put on and deals effectively with any which have been missed by the earlier spraying. In the bag, the population rate is likely to rise much more rapidly than on uncovered plants. Although it increases the cost of the job, it is possible to place one greaseproof bag inside another. This gives a satisfactory reinforcement and is something which some growers have found well worth while.

When putting on the bag it must first be inflated, but do not seal it when it is fully extended. It is best to leave just a little 'pressing space', since by so doing there is less possibility of the bag being caused to heel over and collapse.

The buds for covering should be showing their colour well, and in such a condition that the shape of the petals can just be seen. All unnecessary growth should be removed from the stem under the buds, so that the bags can be fitted on snugly. As a record, date of covering can be written on the bag.

Do not tie the bags too tight and close to the head, or the blooms will become mis-shapen. The bag is blown up as if to be burst, and when the bud is inserted it should be approximately in the middle of the bag which must be properly sealed. This is done by gently moulding the paper around the stem. The neck of the bag is then tied very firmly with string. Two ties ensure firmness, one at the top and one at the bottom of the neck of the bag. These will keep the bag upright and prevent it toppling over as the result of strong winds.

If the corners of the bag are folded over, this will cause the air in the bags to fill out the creases.

The period it is necessary to leave on the bags is influenced by the variety being grown and the time of year. August flowering varieties are usually covered for about three weeks, although the Large Exhibition types will take longer than the medium sized varieties. One can usually be sure that if one bloom is ready of a batch of the same variety, covered on the same day, when all were in the same condition, that all will be ready for cutting at the same time.

It is the long petalled varieties which cause some anxiety to the grower who has bagged the blooms. It will be found, however, that each petal will fall into place, although it is usually a few hours after uncovering before the flower heads assume their proper shape. It is therefore advisable to cut the flowers the evening before show day, to ensure the blooms are in first class order.

The advantage in giving each bagged head a separate support

is that in the event of strong winds the plants are held firmly in the ground. It is always advisable to use the best quality bags rather than 'making do' and the cost involved is not at all high.

All the pale coloured sorts, particularly the white and yellows are quite satisfactory when bagged, but it must be said that with some of the pinks and reds, the covering of the blooms may slightly lighten the colour. If this happens to any marked degree, it could easily result in loss of points on the flower show bench.

Where blooms are not being grown for exhibition purposes, any slight colour variation will not matter.

CHAPTER TWELVE

Garden Pompon and Spray Varieties

WHETHER THEY are known as pompones, pompons, or pompoms, this charming section of the chrysanthemum family has now become established as one of the most popular of flowers for garden decoration, cutting and pot work. They are also ideal for window boxes and tubs. In the wide range of named varieties, there are attractive sorts varying in height from 12 inches to almost 4 feet.

This easy and accommodating plant has proved that it can stand adverse weather conditions; in fact, anyone who has already grown the pompons cannot help being impressed by the performance of the plants, both in times of wet and drought. On occasions when the normal early flowering varieties have been prevented by weather conditions from flowering to full capacity, the pompons have been most colourful. The fact that even under conditions of near neglect they will still bloom is another reason for their continuing to gain in popularity.

Pompons have been grown in Britain for nearly a century, but the original varieties varied in height between 3 and 4 feet, and therefore required staking in the same way as the majority of the early flowering sorts.

During recent years, however, many dwarf pompons have been introduced. This has made the section immensely popular, since they can be grown in the small gardens attached to many of the modern houses, moreover, the colour range is very wide and the habit good.

There are many excellent named varieties growing no more than 12 to 18 inches, a few being only 9 or 10 inches high. Some have blooms less than three quarters of an inch in diameter, others being considerably longer. The flowers of some, too, while

11. Showing a market pack of 'White Hope Valley'

12. *Below:* 'Jack Straw'. Deep yellow. A good year-round variety

13. 'Dawn Star
pure white pom
variety

14. 'Skyline'. An ivory-white formal pompon

being fully double, are more or less flat, others being of a real pompon shape. The flowering period extends from the first week in August until well into October. Placed in suitable containers the flowers look superb and, as with most types of chrysanthemum, the blooms are very long lasting. They will often remain fresh looking for up to three weeks if kept where the atmosphere is not too hot and dry. For bedding, it is possible and I think, best to plant varieties of contrasting colours, although this will really depend on the effect desired and on personal preference. Certainly little beds or blocks of separate colours show up well, especially when one remembers how long and late the plants will usually go on producing colour – the dwarf golden-yellow, Denise for instance, being particularly bright and weather resistant.

Since there is as much as 7 or 8 inches between the height of different varieties, it is not difficult when planting a fairly big bed to arrange the taller sorts in the centre of a round or oblong bed or at the back of a narrow border, and using other slightly less tall varieties to produce a graduating effect.

This means a flowering bed or border ranging from about 10 to 18 inches high. Although there are many first class self-coloured varieties, there are also a lot having two or more colours or shades in each flower.

Some of these, grouped with the plain coloured sorts produce a most pleasing effect. It will be obvious that the shortest growing sorts will flower the earliest. Not only are these very dwarf varieties of charming appearance but many of them have been given attractive names as we shall see later.

It is true that some of the earliest varieties of pompons were not anything very special and they lacked brilliance. That cannot be said about the present-day varieties. When so many of us are looking for trouble-free, dwarf plants, needing neither stopping nor, in most cases staking, these plants fit the bill, which is one reason why they have become so popular with the public parks' departments. The natural spray varieties of pompons are deserving of attention for cutting and planting out, one of their features being that the earliest varieties show colour when many of the other types of summer flowers are passing over.

Propagation of the pompons follows the usual lines. Cuttings can be taken early in the year where it is possible to maintain a greenhouse temperature of 48 to 50 degrees F. It has been found that although they will not be actually harmed, cuttings will not

F

root in lower temperatures. It is dampness rather than cold that causes decay to set in.

Where it is not possible to provide artificial heat, it is unwise to take cuttings before the middle of March, and not then if weather conditions are bad. If a propagating case is available, this encourages quicker rooting. Cuttings should be prepared as for other groups of chrysanthemums. The lower leaves are taken off, without damaging the stems and it is unwise to leave much foliage, since the less there is to support, within reason, the quicker the cuttings will root. Plant them about 2 inches apart in boxes, or in small numbers around the sides of a pot. Use a good soil mixture, sterilised, if disease has been prevalent. A suitable mixture can be made up of equal parts of loam and peat and ½ part of silver sand.

Make sure that the cuttings are in the soil firmly, water them in and keep them, as suggested, in a temperature of around 50 degrees F. Shade from strong sunlight can be provided by placing paper over the cuttings as necessary. Subsequently, the plants are treated in the same way as the early flowering varieties, being put outdoors from the end of April onwards, according to soil and weather conditions.

The plants can also be divided, either when they have finished flowering or in the early spring. Another way of increasing stock is to detach young rooted offsets in the spring and plant them up separately in good, prepared positions.

Apart from growing the dwarf pompons in beds and borders, they are splendid for pots, tubs, window boxes; in fact they will grow and look well in almost every type of receptacle. If the growing points are removed while the plants are small they will develop into really bushy specimens.

There are varieties in abundance and colours to suit all tastes. The following are among the best, but reference should be made to the catalogues of specialist growers for particulars of many other named sorts.

Name	*Colour*	*Height*	*Time of Flowering*
ALLAN RUFF	Chestnut-bronze	12 inches	Late August.
BILLIE BOY	Golden-yellow	12 inches	Early September.
BLONDIE	Orange-bronze	15 inches	Early September.
BRIGHT EYE	Orange, red centre	15 inches	Late August.
BUNTY	White, bronze centre	18 inches	Late August.

Name	Colour	Height	Time of Flowering
CAMEO	Pure white	15 inches	Late August.
CATHIE	Rose-pink (small)	15 inches	August.
CREAM BOUQUET	Cream	12 inches	Early September.
DANNY	Lilac-rose, flushed yellow	18 inches	Early September.
DENISE	Golden-yellow (small)	13 inches	Late August.
FAIRIE	Strawberry-pink	18 inches	Late August.
IMP	Crimson	15 inches	Late August.
JANET	Rich shell-pink	15 inches	Late August.
KIM	Scarlet-bronze	16 inches	Late August.
LILAC DAISY	Lilac-rose	14 inches	August.
PICOLINO	Old gold shaded bronze	16 inches	Late August.
TIPTOE	Gold	12 inches	Early September.
TOMMY TROUT	Amber-bronze	15 inches	August.
WOKING PROFUSION	Yellow flushed bronze	16 inches	Late August.

There are many good named indoor chrysanthemums which are known as spray varieties, making them most valuable for indoor decoration. During the last few years a whole selection of natural, early flowering garden spray varieties have been introduced, and these have already proved most popular. They are easy and trouble free to grow, needing no supports. They produce a wealth of flowers which are not only ideal for garden display but are most valuable for all floral decorative purposes. The main flowering period for all varieties is the whole of September.

During hot, dry weather, these spray varieties and also the pompons will greatly benefit by a mulch of good compost, manure, peat or even straw, although this is really best put down in the early summer. Do not use lawn mowings, which so often harbour flies. These pests soon turn their attention to the plants and can easily spoil them.

Among the best of the summer spray varieties are the following:

ALPHA. White with green centre – unusual appearance. Stands wet weather and will keep for a long period in water when cut.

AUSTIN ROSE. This colour is hard to describe; rose shading to purple before fully out, tint of gold in the centre; robust habit. 3 feet.

BETA. Rose-pink tinted salmon centre. Good habit, strong

upright grower, produces a cluster of flowers at the top; ideal for decorative purposes and also borders. 2 feet 6 inches.

CHATSWORTH. Bright orange-bronze, pointed petals, does not fade. Medium height. Heavy cropper. August.

CHERRY RIPE. Brilliant bright red, one of the best red sprays yet introduced; most suitable for decoration and market work, very heavy cropper. September.

DELTA. Bronze to orange, suitable for cutting, does not damp. Quite different from other colours listed in the section; flowers on thin wiry stems. 3 feet.

GARDEN WHITE. Pure white spray, that is a miniature of the decorative type having small reflexed blooms; most suitable as a garden plant and useful for cutting. Dwarf habit. End of August.

GOLDEN ORFE. Bright golden, true spray, produces a mass of bloom flowering all at the same period. August–September. 3 feet 6 inches.

HILDE. A very beautiful pom with salmon-pink flowers overlaid with a suspicion of red. Fine upright grower.

LILAC DAY. Lilac, with deeper centre shading off to pink, most attractive for border; suitable for cutting and market. 3 feet.

MARKET GROWER. Bronze reflexed, heavy cropper, seedling from Chatsworth, but with longer stems and fuller flower.

NORFOLK. Pastel shade of bronze, very full centre tinted yellow; habit ideal, flowers standing out above plant. 3 feet.

NURSE. Pure white, much admired as a garden plant and also for cutting for decorative purposes. 2 feet 6 inches.

PACKWELL. Deeper and brighter than Chatsworth, longer stems, blooms firm and spiky. Early August.

POWDERPUFF. Soft pastel shade of pink. Ideal for cutting and for decorative display, etc. This colour will blend with almost every flower. Perfect foliage. Has been shown at exhibitions with great success. Flowers early September. 2 feet.

REDSPRAY. Flaming-red with gold reverse, one of the best red sprays for cutting. Admired at all shows; will be in great demand for the garden, also for market work.

ROSESPRAY. Bright rose, gold centre, good foliage; upright grower, ideal for back of borders and most useful for cutting for decoration. This is the only variety of this colour.

THETA. Pale salmon with deep centre; flowers standing out well above foliage, suitable for any artistic work.

WALLY RUFF. Salmon to rose, very tight centres tinted golden, cluster of bloom on short stems. Perfect habit. 2 feet.

WENDY. Clear orange-bronze; excellent habit and growth, heavy cropper, one of the best orange sprays.

CHAPTER THIRTEEN

Koreans and Rubellums

ALTHOUGH the hardy hybrid Korean chrysanthemums are now fairly well known, it was not until 1937 that they were introduced to this country. They have proved to be a great asset, for most of the named varieties are very hardy and usually continue to provide colour after the early flowering garden chrysanthemums have been spoiled by frosts.

It was, in fact, the aim of the originators of the Korean hybrids to raise plants which would bloom outdoors much later than the varieties then in cultivation. This, no doubt, was why they decided to work on *Chrysanthemum coreanum*, a completely hardy flowering plant, hailing from Korea and Siberia.

After years of careful work, a series of well shaped, bushy plants was raised. These were 2 to 2½ feet high and literally covered with showy flowers in a wide colour range. It was some years before the raisers were fully satisfied with their creations, but in 1934 the hardy Korean hybrids were released in the United States of America. Messrs. Wells, the specialist growers of Merstham, secured the British rights for distribution in this country and offered the first varieties in 1937. The original six sorts distributed were Apollo, bronze-red; Diana, pink; Ceres, gold and bronze; Daphne, lilac-pink; Mars, wine-red, and Mercury, salmon-red. These were soon followed by other splendid varieties in many colours.

It was soon noticed that not only were some of the shades of colour new to chrysanthemums, but most flowers had a brilliance and sheen not previously seen. This meant that soon after the introduction of the Korean hybrids they were being grown by many gardeners with great pleasure and satisfaction. Other varieties were introduced in fairly quick succession. It must be said, however, that some of the later sorts do not conform to the original intention of the originators, that all varieties should be perfectly hardy.

The value of the Koreans for indoor decoration is tremendous, for not only does the lustre of their colouring brighten a dull room in the daytime, but it shows to great advantage in artificial light at night. Not only so, for used in conjunction with the autumn foliage and berries of shrubs, they produce a delightful effect, particularly since there are so many beautiful bronze and red shades.

Few, if any, hardy plants require less attention or give such pleasing results, whether seen in the garden or when used for indoor decoration. New plants should be obtained in late April or early May. If they have sufficient moisture, they will soon take hold in their new positions and branch out and produce large quantities of flowers from August onwards.

Although it is not essential to support the plants, it is often helpful to do so, particularly in open situations, for some light supports are a help against strong autumn gales.

According to space available, they may be planted from 18 to 24 inches apart, in good well dug soil. A few of the varieties rarely grow more than 2 feet high, but there are many others which make fine shapely plants up to $3\frac{1}{2}$ feet, while some are even taller. All produce an abundance of cuttings, while established clumps can be divided in the spring, and small pieces planted up separately.

Much the cheapest way of obtaining a stock of the hybrid Korean chrysanthemums is to raise them from seed. A large number of plants of excellent, though varying form, may be expected from a packet of the hybrid strain.

The seed is sown in pans or boxes of good compost during February and March, in a temperature of from 50 to 55 degrees F. Germination is usually quick and regular, and the seedlings should be pricked off early and before they become drawn and spindly. Move them into other pans or seed boxes, and give water as necessary, without making the compost sodden. Gradually harden off the seedlings as they are quite ready to be moved into their flowering positions by early May. It is at this time that it is worth while potting up a few specimens for growing on, to provide colour in the greenhouse or conservatory, where they are always appreciated.

It is not possible to raise plants producing the same colour flowers as the plants from which the seed was saved, but the possibilities are almost limitless, and tremendous pleasure can be obtained by raising Korean chrysanthemums in this way. In addition, there is always the chance that something entirely new or different from existing varieties may turn up. This is a prospect which makes raising plants from seed so exciting.

Many varieties of the Otley Koreans make excellent pot plants for indoor decoration. These succeed particularly well for this purpose if they are grown outdoors in the usual way, and the foliage of the open ground plants is of good colour and often in better condition than that of plants which have been grown in pots from their earliest stages.

The best way to deal with the plants is to carefully lift and pot them in the early autumn when they are fully grown and when the flower buds are just beginning to show colour. For this purpose, use pots of a suitable size to accommodate the roots without having to remove much soil from them. Put some crocks or other drainage material at the bottom, and carefully work in the compost without breaking the roots.

Keep the plants out of direct sunlight for a week or so after planting, but not in dense shade.

Varieties of Otley Koreans which are particularly good for pot work include: Canary, semi-double, fine yellow; Rusty, single, russet-red, and Tawny Owl, double, tawny-orange, darker at centre, producing an effect which resembles the eyes of an owl. Brown Owl is another double, the rich bronze flowers appearing on good high bushes, while Roselea is a real gem for all kinds of decorative and pot work, the double rose-pink blooms being neat and dainty.

A few years ago a new race of early dwarf Koreans was raised and introduced by Mr. Fred M. Simpson. They were named the Otley Korean chrysanthemums, and wherever there is room they are well worth a place in the garden. They do not require staking or stopping, since they grow naturally into compact, bushy plants covered with long lasting flowers. They are ideal for the front of the border, for the rockery or window box, while they make splendid pot plants.

Excepting in warm sheltered districts, it is advisable to give them some protection during the winter. They vary in height from 12 to 24 inches and few of them are less than 14 inches wide, the flowering time extending from August to October, according to variety.

Among the August flowering plants are: Carolyn, double, yellow; Otley Rose, semi-double, rose-pink; Our Jane, single, cyclamen-pink, all 16 inches high and 12 inches wide. Early Jewel, single, brick-bronze, grows 15 by 20 inches. In September there are: Otley Pride, pink; Cardinal, red; Colleen, mauvy-pink; Princess Elizabeth, deep wine; and in October, the following are good: Cherry, magenta, October Charm, deep rose, and Sultan, rich dark red.

There is also a taller growing type of Korean chrysanthemum which produces medium size flowers. Known as the Windsor hybrids, they are excellent for growing as a spray cut flower. Flowering during August and September, the named sorts include: Audrey, pink; Cordelia, salmon-pink with small yellow centre; Hubert, rich scarlet-orange; Petruchio, dusky crimson, and Oswald, terra-cotta. These make plants 2 to 2½ feet high and as much wide, making them very conspicuous in the garden, as well as being first class in the house.

AN INTERPLANTED KOREAN BORDER

I do not think that the value of the Koreans has yet been fully realised, for although a few plants in the herbaceous border always look well, they can be massed with the shorter Michaelmas Daisies to make an effective display. If care is taken over the height of each subject, a marvellous show can be obtained with a wealth of bloom appearing in pleasing colour tones from September and October onwards.

The best effect of all, however, is obtained by making a Korean bed or border, for by judicious selection and planting it is possible to have colour over several months of the year. What are suitable combinations? I have interplanted with ordinary bedding subjects such as nemesia and *Phlox Drummondii* and edged with alyssum and lobelia. These, of course, provide colour from June onwards. I do not think that such plants are entirely satisfactory, and for a bed or border which can be left for two or three years, the spring flowering bedding plants are really best. In this case they are, of course, planted in October when the Koreans are in bloom, so that care must be taken in moving among the plants. It is necessary to plan where the plants are going, and not just push in extra plants regardless of their habit. Properly placed, an attractive display can be secured which will overcome the objection sometimes raised that with chrysanthemums, colour is only available in late summer and autumn, leaving so long a time devoid of a show.

With such a plan given, 2 feet should be allowed all round, thus providing ample room for other subjects to be included. While the plants bush out well, and by the time they flower all the space around them will be taken up, there is still every opportunity for planting to secure a display of colour in the spring and early summer.

As suggestions, the well known spring flowering bedding subjects fit in well, and need, as already indicated, to be planted in the autumn. Wallflowers Blood Red, Cloth of Gold, Fire King and Scarlet Emperor never fail to flower abundantly if really strong, bushy plants are used.

Sweet Williams, too, are quite useful, although rather inclined to be straggly. I prefer wallflowers inter-planted with Myosotis (Forget-me-nots) Royal Blue, which grow 9 inches high. Double red, pink or white daisies, can be used for planting the edges.

In addition, tulips and daffodils fit in well when planted between wallflowers and myosotis, and some of the smaller bulbs such as crocuses and scillas will widen the colour scope and produce a pleasing effect, especially if well placed. All of these plants and bulbs will be over before the Koreans have made much growth in the spring, so that there is no question of competition for light or room. In the plan given the varieties can be changed to suit personal taste, and this applies to any subjects used for interplanting.

The following is a brief colour description of Koreans, selected for their good growth and reliability:

Doubles, all growing about 2½ feet: Caliph, ox-blood red: Immortelle, clear lemon; Peach Caliph, pinkish peach.

Singles 2½ to 3 feet high, Copper Rose, mandarin-pink; Coral Mist, real coral shade; Coral Pink, clear pink; Cornelian, terracotta; Derby Day, burnt-orange; Flame, brick-red; Heyday, cerise; Lammas Day, amber; Oporto, port-wine red; and Saladin, chinese-lacquer red.

Dwarf or cushion Koreans: Little Tuck, 1 foot, yellow and bronze; Belinda, 1 foot, orchid-pink, green centre; Red Riding Hood, terra-cotta; Bo-Peep, pink-bronze; Miss Lockett, lemon-yellow; all growing 18 inches. Alice, old rose; Honey Pot, honey-yellow; Little Miss Muffett, strawberry-pink; Margery Daw, cerise-red; Polly Flinders, mandarin-red, which all grow about 2 feet high.

Of the same height are Anastasia, the old purple-lilac pompon variety and Tommy Tucker, with golden-yellow pompons and bronzy red centres.

Few, if any, plants will give more satisfactory results than these Koreans and none could need less attention, for each year they will bring a blaze of colour to the garden and will stand up to ten degrees of frost without the new flower buds being harmed.

CHRYSANTHEMUM RUBELLUM

It has always been somewhat of a conjecture as to whether the various and often neglected chrysanthemum species would respond to selection or to hybridisation. It is evident that some will, for we have *C. rubellum* to prove it. The origin of this plant remains shrouded in mystery, for neither its beginning nor the way in which it was first introduced to the gardens of Britain is known.

It was in the autumn of 1929 that an unknown plant appeared in the rock garden in the Happy Valley at Llandudno. In an effort to solve its identity, specimens were sent to the Royal Botanic Gardens at Kew in 1933, with a request that they should be named.

Authorities there suggested that the plant was probably *Chrysanthemum erubescens*, a species which was known and which had been described and illustrated in the *Botanical Magazine*. This was the name adopted for the 'new' plant and under which it was exhibited at the Royal Horticultural Society's show held at Olympia on September 25th to 27th, 1935. It was given an Award of Merit and described as 'a lovely species growing about thirty inches tall with soft pink flowers rather like those of a large Michaelmas Daisy'. The introducing of this subject and the honour bestowed upon it by the R.H.S. caused the plant to become a minor sensation in the horticultural world, and it was soon in great demand.

Messrs. Perry, the plant growers of Enfield, acquired a stock of *C. rubellum*, saved seeds and raised a number of seedlings that showed considerable variations from the type. They selected and propagated the best of these, and two that immediately became popular were named Clara Curtis and Anna Hay. Both had the advantage of being sweet scented as is the type plant. Clara

Curtis has small, much divided dark green leaves carried on rather stiff reddish stems. It is of neat bushy habit producing large flowers about 2½ inches in diameter, the deep rose petals showing up well against the central yellow disc.

Anna Hay is very similar in habit, but the flowers are a lovely soft shell-pink colour and are larger than those of Clara Curtis. Both varieties produce good branching sprays of flowers which are very long lasting and excellent for cutting.

Hybridisers soon found that the *C. rubellum* varieties responded well to cross pollination and before long a splendid range of hybrids was raised and distributed. They have provided a wide colour range so valuable for all kinds of floral decoration. With all this success there has not been any loss of hardiness, sturdiness or elegance. All exhibit the fine qualities of the plant first seen at Llandudno, which is the ancestor of all the rubellums in cultivation. This was indeed a rare and valuable find, and one which could be repeated in other directions if we keep our eyes open to see any unusual plant which has obviously outstanding qualities.

C. rubellum and its varieties are quite long lasting but it is a good plan to rejuvenate the stock from time to time. This can be done from cuttings taken in the same way as for the early flowering chrysanthemums.

The culture of these chrysanthemums is very simple. They are not particular as to soil, although they prefer one which is well drained but yet does not dry out during the summer. Of perennial habit, *C. rubellum* and its hybrids are absolutely hardy and will go on giving a bright display for years. It is possible to secure varieties which will provide colour from early August until November and which make a bright show at a time when most of the other perennials have finished blooming.

They do not require disbudding or stopping and very few need any support at all, a few twiggy sticks placed round the plants will keep growth upright and, particularly in open or exposed positions, will prevent damage to the charming flowers from rain or wind.

The planting season extends throughout April and early May, and the young plants should be placed in a sunny position, being firmly embedded in the soil and watered in.

They quickly establish themselves, and quite small plants soon increase in size and give a good display the same year.

Groups of three or more of one variety look best, since the

attractive foliage shows up the gaily coloured blooms much better than if single plants are dotted about the garden.

Apart from Clara Curtis and Anna Hay, other first class named sorts include, Ann, Lady Brocket, apricot-pink, which is particularly long lasting in water, Jessie Cooper, with large bright chestnut-crimson blooms; Duchess of Edinburgh with glowing velvety-red flowers which remain in good condition for several weeks, while Prince Charles makes shapely plants covered with old rose coloured blooms: Princess Margaret is orchid-pink; Wild Honey a marvellous shade of peach-yellow blended with coral; Vagabond Prince, cyclamen-pink overlaid with a mauve sheen, and Red Ensign, Indian-red with a bright yellow centre.

Chrysanthemum rubellum and its varieties make excellent pot plants for both the conservatory and living-room.

It is possible to increase stock by root division or from seed, and although the seedlings raised may not produce flowers anything like the parent plant there is always the possibility of securing something good.

CHAPTER FOURTEEN

Singles and Anemone-centred Varieties

THE MODERN single flowered chrysanthemums are most lovely and are ideal for decorative purposes. The early flowering garden varieties need the same treatment as the outdoor double sorts described in Chapter 10.

They may be grown as spray varieties, in which case all the laterals are retained. The central bud is eventually removed; all the others being retained. In the case of disbudded flowers the central bud only, is 'secured'. If there are a lot of laterals, their number can be reduced in order to encourage bigger individual flowers. As the result of constant careful work by trade growers, present-day single varieties are altogether superior to the older sorts, having many more petals of much better texture, making for an altogether finer flower, with much longer lasting qualities.

To secure late singles of showing quality, they should be treated similarly to the exhibition and decorative sorts, not forgetting the feeding.

The cuttings need not be taken until late January onwards and there is rarely any difficulty in getting them to root well. Some of the older growers always added brick dust to the mixture for rooting the cuttings. This is not easy to obtain but should be used where possible.

The cuttings are usually well rooted within five or six weeks when they can be moved to 3 inch or 60 size pots. Then, as growth proceeds, transfer them to 5 inch and then to 8 or 9 inch pots.

The chief difference in the cultivation of the singles as compared with the other types is that of 'stopping'. Many specialist growers indicate in their catalogues just what should be done with individual varieties. Many of them need not be stopped at all, but some of the strong growing varieties, such as Molly God-frey, Betty Woolman, Broadacre and Desert Song, should be stopped in April. In either case, the buds should be 'secured' early in September. This means that buds seen during August are too early for the late shows or for producing blooms at a time when the earlier flowering kinds have finished.

Too much stopping is liable to lead to some of the flowers becoming double, which might suggest that the supplier had sent the wrong varieties.

For exhibition blooms the grower will have to decide on the number of flowers each plant will carry. For the best quality display, this may be from six to nine, but with some of the extra strong growers a dozen or more can be allowed. With these, the reduction of blooms to a small number leads to rather coarse, full flowers.

The late single varieties are becoming increasingly popular for use in the greenhouse, living-room and for market work. For these purposes one could perhaps allow up to ten blooms if the plants are robust.

As always, it is a good plan to allow one or two more growths than are actually required, to develop. These can be regarded as a reserve in case of accident or damage by earwigs and other insects. At disbudding time, unwanted shoots can be removed.

Some training is advisable, and many growers find it an advantage to tie the plants flat to a little framework of light canes. More plants can then be accommodated in a limited space.

These canes are inserted at the final potting time, and training is started when the plants are on the standing out ground. It is, of course, also possible to grow the late singles as ordinary pot plants, by inserting one or two supports and looping the growths with raffia or soft string.

As with other pot plants, feeding can commence about the end of July. There are a number of good proprietary fertilisers which can be used or made up. Care should be taken to carry out the manufacturers' instructions.

Watering is a job to be done regularly, and while every other day may be regarded as a guide to frequency, in hot weather the plants may need water daily. Do not wait until the flower buds are seen before beginning to feed, but give fairly weak feeds at an early stage in order to help to build up good growths. It is strong healthy growth that is going to produce good blooms.

Top dressing is also needed by pot plants and is usually given two or three times during the season, the first one being applied about the second week in August. For this use equal parts of well screened or sifted loam and old manure, plus about a cupful of chrysanthemum fertiliser, such as Woolmans and Bentleys, or seaweed fertilisers such as Neptune's Bounty, which is most reliable, to each peck of loam and manure.

A mixture of all these should be placed in the top of the soil in the pot, say about ½ inch deep. This, of course, is why the soil in the pots was finished off low when the final potting was done. Such top dressings should be given as a replacement of one of the regular liquid feeds so as not to provide too much rich fare at one time. Disbudding should be done gradually in order to avoid any check. It is the regular spraying, tying in and feeding that brings the finest results.

ANEMONE-CENTRED

Although anemone-centred chrysanthemums have been known and grown in America for quite a long time, they have never been particularly popular in this country. During the last few years they have become better known and their value for decoration is now being appreciated.

The flowers are quite different from any other type, since they have a limited number of ray florets which surround a cushion of disc florets, most of which appear as prominent tubular structures. A wide colour range is available, and in many instances the disc and ray florets contrast attractively in colour as well as appearance. In some respects the anemone-centred varieties can be regarded as singles, in which the central or disc florets are raised and made more prominent.

Cultivation, too, is the same as for the single varieties. Cuttings are inserted in February or March, being potted up when rooted and then moved on until the young plants reach the 7½ or 8 inch size. It is rarely, if ever, necessary to give bigger pots, for the root system made by this section is considerably thinner and smaller than that of the other types. For ordinary greenhouse or living-room decoration, it is not necessary to stop the plants. For exhibition work, however, the anemone-centred varieties should be treated in a similar way to the greenhouse singles. This means giving them two stops and flowering them on the second crown buds. The exact time of these stoppings will depend on the condition of the plants, but generally speaking it will be about the

15. Spoon Chrysanthemums. For garden or pots

16. Chrysanthemum
'White Spider'. This
has strong stems and
good foliage

17. An exhibition display, showing flower arrangement
value of Chrysanthemums

middle of March. Then, two (or three, if the plant is very strong) growths should be taken up. Stop these shoots about the middle of June, letting two or three breaks grow on for flowering.

There are both tall and dwarf varieties, some of the latter being excellent as pot plants. When disbudded, really good sized individual blooms will develop, but when allowed to break naturally and flower as sprays, the result is most pleasing. There are large and medium flowered sorts, blooming during November and requiring little heat; they can be treated in their later stages of growth in exactly the same way as the mid-season and late flowering decoratives, with the advantage that they thrive in a rather lower temperature.

As will be seen from Chapter 20 the anemone-centred varieties are classified as Section VII in the National Chrysanthemum Society's regulations. Particularly good in pots are the following: Beautiful Lady, shell-pink, creamy-white cushion; Cassino, deep rose-pink, pale pink cushion; Freda, deep pink, yellow cushion; Raymond Mounsey, crimson, lighter centre, and Thora, rose, creamy centre.

SINGLE CHRYSANTHEMUMS (GREENHOUSE)

These single-eyed daisy type of flowers are either grown as sprays, that is letting all the flowers on each shoot develop, or disbudded to one flower per stem as with the other types. The flowering period is November and December and the culture and general habit similar to the decoratives.

ALBERT COOPER	Large yellow; fine flower. Highly recommended. 4 feet.
BEDOUIN	An orange-amber flower after the style of Desert Song but more easily grown. A fine exhibition single. 4 feet.
CLEONE	Pale pink; large flower. 4½ feet.
DESERT SONG	One of the finest singles. Fawn terracotta with gold tips. 3½ feet. November–December.
FIREBIRD	Very striking. Bright orange-flame with a golden ring in the centre immediately catches the eye. 4 feet.
FIRECREST	A beautiful colour combination, bright flame, each petal tipped yellow. A.M. 1952. 4 feet.

G

FLAREPATH | A bright crimson with a small eye. Petals neatly laid, a fine exhibition flower on a strong stem. 4½ feet.

MASON'S BRONZE | Orange-bronze medium single, very free, strong growth, excellent for decoration.

PEGGY STEVENS | Large golden-yellow. A.M. 1955.

PREFERENCE | Large clear pink with small eye. Neat foliage. A.M. 1955.

PRETTY | A lovely pink for exhibition or market. A.M. 4 feet.

WOOLMAN'S GLORY | One of the best singles introduced. May be likened to a terra-cotta bronze Desert Song. Large refined flower.

ANEMONE-CENTRED AND POMPON GREENHOUSE VARIETIES

This particularly attractive anemone-centred type has, since the war, become increasingly popular. They are delightful for decoration, the colour combinations displayed being notable, and seem to combine the grace and lightness of the single flower, with the strength and solidity of the double decorative types in a most pleasing manner. Culture is similar to that of the decoratives and November singles. The main difference between these and singles, is that they have a centre full of small petals making a cushion instead of the open eye of the ordinary single flower.

AMBER LONG ISLAND BEAUTY | A striking sport from the well known anemone-centred variety. A truly luminous tangerine-amber. Perfect for decoration.

BEAUTIFUL LADY | Delicate pink, with creamy-white cushion, dwarf habit.

CHRISTMAS GOLD | Golden-yellow, December.

DENEBOLA | Lilac-pink with deeper cushion.

KING OF PLUMES | Yellow thread-petalled flower.

LONG ISLAND BEAUTY | Large flower, pure white, with yellow centre, very striking.

PINK LONG ISLAND BEAUTY | Pink sport, good habit.

RAYMOND MOUNSEY	Reddish-crimson petals, large cushion, flecked with light bronze.
YELLOW GRACELAND	Yellow sport from Graceland.

EARLY FLOWERING SINGLES FOR THE GARDEN

These are ideal for bedding purposes or a mass display. No stopping or disbudding is necessary.

DOREEN WOOLMAN	Intense golden-orange, September.
FEATHERS	Pretty, rolled-petalled white, weather resistant. Ideal for garden bedding. 2 feet.
JEAN	Orange terra-cotta, very fine.
MAJOR ROBERTSON	Crimson-scarlet, large flower. August.
NECTAR	Almond-blossom pink, free blooming, in sprays. September.
PREMIÈRE	Anemone-centred. An attractive bright yellow with solid cushion of same colour. Really good. 3 feet.
SEPTEMBER GEM	Clear yellow, in huge clusters on fine stems. September.
SHIRLEY CRIMSON	Rich intense crimson with golden disc.
YELLOW CHARM	Bright yellow of dwarf habit. Withstands bad weather. 3 feet.

CHAPTER FIFTEEN

Exhibition mid-season and late flowering Decorative Varieties

THERE IS ALWAYS a sense of achievement when one is able to produce flowers at times when they are relatively scarce. This is one of the reasons why it is worth growing the mid-season and late flowering varieties of chrysanthemums. These, of course, come into bloom when weather conditions will have spoiled the outdoor flowering kinds, and they therefore need the protection of a greenhouse.

Whether plants are lifted from the open ground or are in pots they will have to be housed when bad weather appears imminent. The exact time for this depends on the season. The mid-season varieties are normally given cover towards the end of September, but the really late flowering sorts can be left in the open until the second or even third week in October so long as frost does not threaten.

A clean start under glass must be ensured. This can be done by removing all the remains of the previous crop and giving the house a thorough cleaning and fumigating. The plants themselves should be drenched with a good protective insecticide-fungicide.

No matter how sound a plant has been built up during the previous months, by good growing and balanced nutrition, the buds still need looking after if they are to produce really good quality blooms. Also growth must remain disease and pest free. Close conditions in the greenhouse are conducive to mildew and aphis. The plants must be spaced so that air can circulate freely between them. Crowding the greenhouse will invite mildew and make proper watering difficult. The sun can sometimes be quite strong through glass in October, and some kind of shading should be available. Both muslin and polythene are useful.

After housing, carefully controlled feeding can be continued, but it is important to know what to use and how to apply it. As we have seen elsewhere, the general principle of feeding chrysanthemums is to supply nitrogen during the active growth phase, with increased potash and phosphates after the buds have been secured, so that it is the latter type of feeding, which is needed by housed plants.

Bulky organics are clearly of little use at this stage of growth, but whatever is applied must be easily soluble and provide balanced nutrition from the time of application.

For the first few weeks after housing the plants should have plenty of ventilation both by day and night, but as the flowers begin to unfold, care is needed in avoiding fluctuations in temperature, and during sunny days some kind of shading may be needed again.

High temperatures are not required at any time, but there must be sufficient warmth to exclude dampness. This is why care is necessary in regulating the heater. Large Exhibition varieties, in particular, need a buoyant atmosphere for they are the most susceptible to petal damping. It is a mistake to wait until severe frost threatens before giving heat at night. The blooms are most likely to be spoiled by mild, damp weather.

Many growers find it an advantage to fumigate the plants every week or ten days. Although this is not essential, it certainly is a good way of getting rid of pests before they settle on the blooms and spoil them.

While surplus water running on to the floor will do no harm for the first fortnight after housing, once the buds begin to open, moisture must be reduced to the minimum. If the greenhouse has a concrete floor on which the pots are standing, it is advisable to mop up any surplus water.

Sometimes plants lifted from the open ground droop a little when brought into the greenhouse. This is only a temporary condition, and given a little shading, they soon look perky again.

There are three distinct periods of flowering for greenhouse chrysanthemums, October, November and December. There are many varieties which will flower well in October with little or no heat at all. It is important, however, to prevent stagnant as well as cold air remaining in the house.

If the stools are being retained as stock plants for propagating for the next season, they must not be neglected at the end of their flowering period. They should be cut down to about 12 or 14 inches from the base and less water given to the compost. It will not be long before the new shoots begin to develop, and it is these, of course, which provide the cuttings for the following year. Here, perhaps, is a good place to say that the roots should be given a thorough watering three days before it is intended to take the cuttings.

The lists that follow will give a good indication of the tremendous range of varieties available, and new ones are being added every season. It is, therefore, advisable to consult the catalogues of the specialist growers to see what new varieties are introduced each season. To give a very long list of varieties here would not only take up more space than is available, but such a list would become out of date before long.

The section for long known as Japanese chrysanthemums has now been re-classified as Large Exhibition although many growers still refer to these varieties as 'Japs'. They are, perhaps, a little more difficult to cultivate than the other late flowering sorts, and generally speaking the very large blooms are not really suitable for use in living-rooms. They are, however, superb for exhibition. They need a long season of growth, and cuttings should be taken from late December onwards. If these are inserted where there is a temperature of about 50 degrees F., the rooted cuttings should be ready for their first potting by mid-February. The plants should be in their final 10 inch pots before the end of May.

Most growers of greenhouse chrysanthemums endeavour to have some blooms available at Christmas when they are highly valued. This is possible with a number of varieties among which are the following: White Favourite and its coloured sports, Shirley Late Red, Balcombe Perfection, Fred Shoesmith, American Beauty and Lilian Richford.

For this purpose, the plants can be grown in pots or planted in wire baskets and kept in the open ground until late September. Alternatively, they can be grown from late struck cuttings in 5 or 6 inch pots. They must not lack moisture during the summer months.

EXHIBITION (JAPANESE) VARIETIES

ALBERT BARNES   Incurving Japanese. The petals curl and interlace making a solid bloom of chestnut-red with bronze reverse. 4½ feet.

ALBERT SHOESMITH — A magnificent incurving yellow. Easy to grow. 4 feet.

BIRMINGHAM — A fine crimson gold reverse.

CHARLES WOOLMAN — Long petals make a deep flower of great size. Long lasting qualities, strawberry-rose with ivory reverse.

CHRISTINE WOOLMAN — An incurving Japanese of unusual colour. An attractive salmon with buff reverse. Good quality and size. 4½ feet.

CONNIE MAYHEW — A beautiful primrose coloured incurving flower, making a large ball.

COSSACK — Shining crimson – one of the best. Dwarf habit. F.C.C.

DUKE OF KENT — One of the largest whites in existence. Dwarf habit, reflexing flower.

FLORENCE WOOLMAN — An unusual colour, buff shading to green in the centre. Very attractive and a fine flower of incurving type.

GREEN GODDESS — One of the most outstanding introductions of recent years. A pretty sea-green with a luminous quality which shows up to advantage under artificial light. The flower is solid, wide and deep, of excellent size and beautifully finished. Can also be grown as a decorative carrying 4–5 blooms per plant on a natural 1st. crown. A.M. 4½ feet.

PRINCESS ANNE — Pretty light pink tinted salmon.

RED CHEER — Attractive scarlet-crimson with gold reverse. Firm rolled petals being very resistant to damping. Pretty for decoration. 4 feet. Seedling from Birmingham.

SENATOR — A bright red reflexed decorative, with an attractive gold reverse for exhibition or cut flower. A.M. 4 feet.

SNOWCAP — Reflexed white, building up a solid flower. Excellent keeping variety. A.M.

SUSAN ALESWORTH — Deep pink with silver reverse incurving.

SYMBOL — A large rich orange-bronze. Excellent for exhibition.

WOKING SCARLET — Medium reflexed of a pretty scarlet crimson. Ideal for decoration. 3½ feet.

MID-SEASON DECORATIVE VARIETIES

APRICOT MY LADY — A pretty apricot-salmon sport. Neat reflexed flowers. Excellent for exhibition.

APRICOT PRINCESS ANNE — An attractive sport from this well known variety, the same habit as its parent.

AUTUMN TINTS — A bright bronze. Wide reflexing petals and vigorous growth. Strong stems. Oct.–Nov. 4½ feet.

AVRIL DOIG — Deep strawberry. Hard petalled flowers very neat and full centred. Grown on 2nd. crown; good for Christmas.

BALCOMBE PERFECTION — Amber-bronze, broad petalled flowers. 4½ feet.

BERYL TURTON — Clear pink ball of large size and excellent quality. Has a shine which makes it immediately noticeable in an exhibit. 5 feet.

FLORENCE SHOESMITH — A top class exhibition decorative, very large flower of an intense crimson. A.M.

FRANCES HARRIS — Attractive flower of pretty silvery-pink colour on good stems. For exhibition or decorative work. End of Oct.–Nov. 4½ feet.

FRED SHOESMITH — White with cream centre. A bloom of firm texture and substance. A.M.

MARIE BRUNTON — Deep yellow tinged with orange, tightly incurving flowers with dark green foliage.

MAYFORD CRIMSON — A first class decorative, large size.

MAYFORD PERFECTION	A slightly incurving flower of large size. Colour warm salmon, overlaid apricot.
OPAL QUEEN	An unusual new colour in decorative chrysanthemums, rosy-purple, but with an unmistakable sheen of blue, particularly under artificial light. Reflexed. 4 feet.
ORANGEMAN	A wonderful colour especially for decoration. A particularly pretty orange, the reflexed petals really shine. Medium size dark foliage adds to the effect. End Oct. to early Nov. $4\frac{1}{2}$ feet.
PIONEER	Vivid orange-bronze of exceptional form. A very fine reflexed bloom. Good foliage. $3\frac{1}{2}$ feet.
HAROLD HABGOOD	Probably the best yellow Japanese yet raised. A magnificent huge ball reminding one of Shirley Primrose, only a brighter yellow. Broad petals. A.M. 1958.
JAFFA	Colour, orange terra-cotta; huge flower of numerous petals. F.C.C.
JESSIE HABGOOD	White, well shouldered flower. Very free from damping. F.C.C.
LILAC PRINCE	A soft lilac-pink, broad incurving and interlacing petals. A large ball-shaped flower. Very good for exhibition.
MAJESTIC	Golden-amber; dwarf sturdy habit.
MARGARET SHOESMITH	A large incurving Jap of a pretty shell-pink.
MIGRANT	A promising incurving bronze Jap. Large solid flowers. Will hold its own for exhibition.
PETER MAY	A fine exhibition variety with a large neatly finished reflexed flower after the style of Majestic. The colour is outstanding, a rich purple with wine shadings.
SHIRLEY LAVENDER	The clear lavender petals curling and interlacing. Solid bloom of considerable depth. A good keeper. 4 feet.

SHIRLEY PRIMROSE A giant flower with long petals, one of the largest Japs. F.C.C.

SYLVIA SANKER A true crimson Jap. After the style of Henry Woolman with a neat broad top and square flower of good size, the gold reverse setting off the bright colour. 4½ feet.

CHAPTER SIXTEEN

Cascade and Charm Chrysanthemums

ALTHOUGH it was not until 1933 that the Cascade chrysanthemums were introduced into Britain, they have been known and grown in Japan for a very long time. The Cascade is a free flowering type of small single chrysanthemum, which is unique from a decorative point of view, because it can be trained to produce a solid sheet of colour as much as 2 feet broad and up to 4 feet long. Properly trained, the growths fall downwards from the pot like a waterfall. The plants can also be trained to grow in pillar and bush forms.

They can be raised from seed or cuttings, and plants are sometimes obtainable. The seed is sown in February and March in gentle heat under glass. As soon as the seedlings can be handled, they should be pricked out into boxes or straight into small pots and potted up in the ordinary way.

The young plants should be stopped at the third or fourth leaf, but no further stopping; specimens can, however, be given an additional stopping. If you are growing the plants as bushes, they will easily make branching specimens of 3 to 4 feet high, and when they are in their final pots they can be fed regularly with a good chrysanthemum fertiliser of organic origin.

If plants are grown as bushes for the first year, it will be possible to pick out the best plants for growing on. This is a great advantage, so that the intricate work of training in the cascade or pillar shapes is not wasted on poor material, since the colours do not come true from seed.

While it is not everyone who likes the idea of a trained chrysanthemum, the cultivation of the Cascades can bring a peculiar sense of satisfaction to the grower, especially when he remembers that it all started with a tiny seed.

Then, of course, there is great pleasure to be derived from showing such trained specimens to friends and acquaintances, for well grown plants cannot fail to impress even the person only mildly interested in chrysanthemums.

For seed sowing, use a fairly light compost such as 2 parts of loam and 1 part each of leaf mould and silver sand, while a sprinkling of lime will be of help in encouraging good development. The absence of manure in the seed compost ensures that a good root system is formed before there is a lot of top growth.

As the result of several moves into bigger size pots, as growth proceeds, by early or mid-May the plants should be in their final 9 or 10 inch receptacles. Very often larger pots are needed, or failing pots, square boxes are satisfactory. As soon as the weather is congenial, the plants can be moved outside to an open sunny, but sheltered place. Put them on a hard base so that worms and soil pests cannot enter the pots.

A really rich mixture is advisable for the final potting, and it is best to stick to organic manures for the real feeding matter. Old, decayed sheep and cow manure have been found to be especially valuable.

When the plants are 8 or 9 inches high and after they have been reduced to one or two leading shoots, they will begin to grow more rapidly. It is at this stage that the training must begin. For growing the plants in the Cascade form, they are placed on a shelf, or they can, of course, be stood there at first instead of placing them at ground level as previously advised. Each leader is tied to a bamboo cane or similar support which has been fixed firmly and carefully into each pot at an angle of 45 degrees to the vertical.

Needless to say, the shelf used must be strong, fairly wide and firmly fixed. There should, for preference, be a wall or hedge at the back, and the shelf should be at least 5 feet above ground level to allow the falling growths to develop. For safety, fix a couple of battens across the front of the shelf and wedge each pot so that it cannot move in any direction.

Then drive a bamboo cane into the ground opposite each pot and tie it to the pot at an angle just off the perpendicular. Along this, the leading shoot or shoots have to be trained. This needs care in order not to break the growths. To begin with, you need merely bend the shoots towards the stake with a long loop of raffia. Then the shoots are gradually pulled in and tied every few inches as growth proceeds. The necessary stopping and tying means that the plants need attention every few days.

All laterals or side shoots are stopped at two or three leaves and subsequently as required, in order to make the necessary bushy growth. The leaders are allowed to grow on and are kept tied to the bamboo stake. The plants can be fed throughout the training stage, and right up until the flower buds show colour. Since the plants will grow quickly, the tying in of the leaders must be done frequently while they remain pliable.

The process of pinching back the laterals continues until the buds begin to form. This is usually about mid-September when the growths will be from 4 to 6 feet long.

Where it is quite impossible to put up a shelf from which to train the growths, the pots can remain standing on a hard base against a south facing wall or hedge, with the cane pointing north. The growths will have to be trained upwards until the plants are taken under glass about mid-September, when they are bent downwards. Do not leave this too late or the stems will be too hard and woody to bend.

When taken indoors, the plants are set on the staging or shelf and the growths trained towards the floor.

The removal of the plants is not always an easy job if there is to be no damage to the growths. These must, of course, be untied for transportation. The bamboos cannot be shifted with the pots.

Once in the greenhouse, it is advisable to run a length of battens along the floor and stretch wires or strings from this on to the staging and then on to the rims of the pots. Tie the growths to the wires making sure that the pots are properly supported and that there is no undue strain on any of the growths. The flowering season usually commences in September, going on until December. It is, of course, possible to build up quite an elaborate trellis work, and it is not unknown for well trained plants to be 4 feet or more wide with a length of 8 feet and upwards. Such plants, however, can only be secured after a lot of careful training.

If you do not wish to train the plants into cascades, they can be made into other shapes. These include standards. To secure them, a good strong stake must be inserted right to the bottom of the pot when the final potting is being done. It is up this support that the leader is trained and eventually it will have to support the head of the plant.

The main shoot must be allowed to grow to about 2 feet and have all side shoots removed. At that height, the leader is stopped.

This will give rise to side shoots which in turn are stopped and re-stopped as growth develops. By this means a mop-like head will be produced. The plants are kept outdoors during this process. They must, of course, be well supported so that the wind does not blow the pots over, especially once the head has developed. Move the plant indoors about the middle of September.

As a variation from the standard, the plants can be trained into an 'umbrella' shape. When the leader reaches the height of $2\frac{1}{2}$ feet, the side shoots are encouraged to develop by the regular stopping of the laterals. A high wire umbrella-shaped frame about 3 feet in diameter, is fixed to the top of the support and the side shoots are tied down to this frame. The idea is to cover the whole of the frame by mid-September when stopping ceases.

A slight variation of this method in that the wire frame used is smaller, being only 12 to 15 inches in diameter, produces a 'weeping' form of plant, the leaders spreading over the frame and then hanging down to 'weep'. To secure a well shaped plant, strings can be run at evenly spaced intervals from the edge of the frame to the top of the pot, and leaders are trained down the strings, which can be carefully removed when the plants are coming into flower.

A rather more elaborate training scheme is to make a fan shaped specimen. For this, two plants are put in one pot at the final potting, also three strong bamboo canes, one in the centre and one each side, are placed in a fan shaped position, thus giving a wide angle at the top. These canes form the foundation for the thinner canes, which are placed horizontally, 6 inches apart, starting a few inches above the pot. To obtain a fan shaped specimen, the bottom horizontal cane should be at least 6 feet long, each succeeding cane being slightly shorter, building up into the shape of a fan or half circle. After the plants have had their first stop, when a few inches high, the aim must be by regular stopping and training to get as many leaders and laterals as are needed to fill all the spaces to create the desired design.

Apart from all of these possible shapes into which Cascade chrysanthemums can be trained, they can, of course, be grown as ordinary bushy plants. For this, they are given one stopping while they are small to ensure branching. Plants 3 to 4 feet high covered with lovely blooms can look most impressive at all times.

With regard to the Charm chrysanthemums, they are grown in exactly the same way as the Cascades in the early stages. They were first introduced by Sutton and Sons in 1947, when specimens 2 to 3 feet in diameter, 18 inches high, exhibited at various horticultural shows, caused no small stir. The plants were covered with small single flowers about the size of Michaelmas Daisies. The colour range is now quite wide, taking in shades of red, pink, yellow, bronze and white. They have a delicate scent and the finely cut foliage is in keeping with the habit of the plants. The plants are easy to raise from seed, and they are vigorous growing and of a bushy habit.

To grow really good specimens, seeds should be sown in heat in February, and when the seedlings can be handled they should be pricked out into 3 inch pots. As soon as the third or fourth leaf has formed, the growing point should be removed. No further stopping is necessary, and since the plants develop into sturdy, upright specimens, no supports are required. As they grow, the plants should be moved to 5 inch pots, and by the end of May or early June, they will be ready for their final pots. These will be the 8, 9 or 10 inch size, according to the condition of the plants at that time, and to the size of plants required.

Once in their final pots, stand the plants outdoors on a hard base in a sheltered place so that they are not spoiled by winds. Towards the end of September, move the plants to the cool greenhouse. While they can be kept for a time in a cold house, there is always the possibility that without a buoyant atmosphere, mildew will develop. Wherever the plants are kept, they must have free ventilation. They must be fed regularly, for they are gross feeders, and apart from liquid manure at weekly intervals top dressings of rich soil are needed in order to obtain the finest results, but liquid feeding should stop about the middle of September.

It is also possible to obtain really good, if smaller plants, by sowing seeds early in April in the cold greenhouse or garden frame. The seedlings are pricked off into 3 inch pots and subsequently moved to the 5 inch, or 6 inch size in the case of extra strong plants. These are the pots in which they will flower. If the pots are plunged, up to their rims, in peat, leaf mould or weathered ashes, it will prevent the compost in the pots from drying out, and this, of course, will also save watering. Occasionally in warm, sheltered districts and in good weather, plants can be flowered in the open ground. This is something on which more work could very well be done, with the aim of introducing an outdoor bedding strain.

The plants will need spraying from time to time, and a watch must be kept for the usual chrysanthemum pests.

CHAPTER SEVENTEEN

Lifting and Housing Plants

ALL GARDENERS who have grown chrysanthemums will know how long the plants remain in flower, and 4 months of colour from them is not unusual. The time eventually arrives, however, when in October, the frosts come and the flowers become discoloured, if not spoiled. Fortunately, this need not be the end of the chrysanthemum season, indeed, as we shall see from another chapter, all the year round chrysanthemums are now a possibility. While many of us may wonder if this is a good thing, it is certainly possible to prolong the flowering season until well after Christmas.

For this, a greenhouse is needed, but not a lot of heat is required; in fact, some can be grown without any, so that it is not an expensive job to grow the plants for winter blooming. Even when the weather remains fairly mild in October, the flowers of outdoor sorts are almost certain to be marked by winds and rains.

The exhibition incurved, decorative and late single varieties for greenhouse flowering are propagated, potted and grown in their early stages in exactly the same way as the outdoor sorts. They are either placed in large pots, kept in the open frame or a sheltered position during the summer, or are planted in the open ground.

One of the advantages of growing them in pots is that there is no check, as occurs with the 'lifted' varieties, and even, steady growth does help in producing perfect blooms. The large porous clay pots are the most widely used and, I think, easily the best containers for the plants. Some growers, however, use concrete and even metal receptacles with success. It does seem that if the compost is right, the chrysanthemum is quite tolerant of non-porous 'pots'.

18. *Chrysanthemum maximum* 'T. E. Killen'

19. *Below: Chrysanthemum maximum* 'Jenifer Read'

20. *Above: Chrysanthemum maximum* 'Cobham Gold'

21. *Chrysanthemum maximum* 'Melissa'

While pot grown plants will almost always produce the best blooms, there are still many growers who plant the late flowering sorts directly into the open ground and lift them in the early autumn. As one way of lessening the check of transplanting, the plants are sometimes put into wire baskets, which are buried into the soil. These baskets are available from garden sundriesmen, the usual size being 7 or 8 inches wide and 5 inches deep, and their use reduces root disturbance and the flagging of the leaves, which usually occurs with open ground plants. This method is particularly useful on the heavier types of soil, where the root system is likely to be more compact than in light, sandy loams.

Whether planted in wire baskets or in the open ground, the site must be well prepared and should be no less thoroughly moved and enriched than recommended for the early flowering varieties. If a good dusting of bone meal, about 3 to 4 ounces to the square yard, is worked into the surface soil in June, it will encourage healthy growth.

Varieties for flowering in October and November are usually, but not always, stopped twice. Once, about the end of March, to induce good laterals, and again towards the end of June. This should result in six, or more, good flowering stems. For the December varieties, a second stop is normally given well into July. With all of these, some disbudding may be necessary, this largely depending on the number and size of the flowers required. However good the treatment, the blooms from lifted plants are not likely to be quite so good as those kept in pots.

About the middle of September, the glasshouse soil and the structure itself should be well prepared to receive the plants.

It is a mistake to rush the plants into the house with the remains of a tomato or some other crop, still lying about. While it may be that all troubles of the tomato and other plants are not common to chrysanthemums, some are, including the virulent botrytis diseases. Therefore, remove roots, bits of stems, leaves and other rubbish.

Of greenhouse pests likely to be carried over, white fly is very persistent and can soon become established during mild spells if precautions are not taken. Red spider is not usually a winter pest but cannot be ignored as early as September. Steps should be taken to deal with these possible pests as outlined in Chapter 28.

After tomatoes, the greenhouse border will require little in the way of preparation, since it is likely that the soil will have a fairly high humus content from the old manure previously used. It

H   *113*

should however, be well moved, up to a depth of 9 inches, and if the subsoil is dry, a thorough watering must be given before the plants are housed.

One benefit resulting from a good watering is that it will help to create something approaching the humidity of atmosphere to which the plants have been accustomed out of doors. Close, dry air conditions at housing time must be avoided.

The conditioning of the glasshouse is of far greater importance than is often realised, and nothing is more unhelpful than to bring the plants into a dry, hot atmosphere. This, of course, applies whether one is dealing with 'lifted' or pot grown plants. The temporary wilting of the plants due to root severance, adds to the possibility of mildew, if air conditions are wrong.

A week or two before lifting, it is a good plan to cut some of the roots, by inserting a spade to its full depth, about 9 inches from the stem working in a circle. If half the circle is cut one week and the remainder the next, and if the soil is thoroughly wet when the job is done, there will be little check to the plants. They will then lift easily, with a good ball of soil.

Some growers remove the lower leaves from the plants before lifting them, as well as doing any necessary disbudding. Unwanted side shoots, basal growths and weeds in the pots should also be taken off. One advantage of removing the lower leaves is that the air is able to circulate freely around the plants when they are placed fairly closely together in the greenhouse, and this lessens the possibility of mildew.

In most cases, too, these lower leaves have done their job and would soon yellow off, and possibly become botrytis infected in the ground-level shade of the glasshouse. At one time, it was customary to spray the plants thoroughly with a combined insecticide-fungicide mixture. This, however, makes housing a messy job, and it is easier and, I think better, to spray once the plants are inside.

Having made sure that the soil is really moist, the plants are carefully lifted, keeping as much soil as possible on the roots – a flat tined fork is excellent for this job. It is advisable to keep the plants upright all the time since the ball of soil is more likely to break if the plants lie or fall over on their sides. Trim off any very long or bruised roots. Every plant must be moved with care, for the loss of flower buds can be expensive when one considers the value of each bloom. If the plants have to be moved for some distance the safest way is to use a trolley.

In the greenhouse, take out a trench a foot wide and about as much deep, and have this quite ready when the plants are lifted. Place the plants upright in the trench, grasping them near the base when doing so. Work in fine soil among the roots and gently firm it with the foot. Then give a thorough watering, which helps to bring the soil into close contact with all the roots, finishing off with another layer of soil.

Although chrysanthemums can be placed fairly closely in the greenhouse, they should not touch one another. Keep them well watered, including overhead sprayings, and to lessen the possibility of wilting foliage, the house can be kept closed for a day or two, by which time the leaves will be firm again. Once they are turgid, give them plenty of air and cool conditions. If frost seems imminent, close the ventilators at night. As the weather becomes colder, less ventilation will be needed and the grower will have to decide when it is necessary to provide a little heat, in order to prevent the damping of the petals. Watch must be kept to ensure that mildew or pests do not gain a hold, which they might do if air conditions are bad. It is not necessary to have a temperature higher than about 50 to 55 degrees F., in fact, there are many varieties which do well without any artificial heat, so long as ventilation is satisfactory. Wherever possible, however, just a little artificial warmth will provide the desirable buoyant atmosphere and keep mildew and damping from becoming troublesome.

For convenience in moving among the plants, it is advisable to allow a path of 12 to 18 inches at intervals of 4 feet, whether the rows are long or short. Although cane supports will have been given to the plants outdoors, there is no need for stakes in the greenhouse, since growth will be upright. If the plants on the outside of the bed tend to hang over, a couple of strands of cord fixed to corner posts will put matters right.

When the plants have been well established, they must be kept watered as necessary. A good liquid fertiliser, which is quick acting and has a high potash content, can be given at seven day intervals. This will provide nourishment leading to good sturdy growth, but such feeding must stop once the colour shows in the buds.

There is no need to apply protective spraying unless mildew appears, although occasional fumigation with smoke generators will stop possible advances by caterpillars and thrip. Nicotine shreds, used in accordance with directions, will prevent aphides from gaining a hold.

While it is true that some varieties stand lifting and replanting better than others, a very large number will respond well to this treatment. It is the vigorous growing sorts which make a good root system and have medium sized foliage and pliable stems that seem most able to withstand the check of lifting.

The following is just a short list of varieties which have proved very satisfactory when transferred from the open ground to the greenhouse.

October flowering
Blanche du poitou, dwarf habit, white.
Cranford Yellow, upright grower, bright yellow.
October Red, reliable, crimson gold reverse.
Snowdon, sturdy, unblemished white.

November flowering
Balcombe Perfection, bronze   Crensa, cerise.
Enton Beauty, crimson and gold   Loveliness, silvery-lilac.
In Memoriam, reflexed crimson   Rose Chochod, mauvy-rose.

December flowering
Apricot May Wallace, apricot   December Bronze, bronze.
Favourite, white   May Wallace, pink.
Monument, white   Imperial Pink, pink.
Sussex Red, red   Shirley Brilliant, crimson.
Golden Favourite, yellow   Magoya, clear yellow.

While it is usual to grow many of these lifted plants for spray flowering, it is possible, especially with the December varieties, to disbud. Quite good blooms can be obtained with these later sorts, since they have a longer time to develop.

There is no doubt that flowers of quite good quality can be obtained from plants grown in the open ground and moved to the greenhouse in the autumn. Since the use of pots is unnecessary, it is less costly, while the need for watering during the summer is very much reduced. In some seasons it is not required at all.

Although, of course, there is the question of cost to remember, the growing of the plants in wire baskets or wire pots, as already mentioned, is well worth considering. The minimum of summer care is needed and the quantity of the flowers grown in this way is much higher and certainly, where blooms are marketed, a considerably better price will be obtained. If the baskets are looked after, they will be usable for several seasons.

One thing which is very noticeable with all lifted plants, is that in the normal way the foliage is of excellent colour and good condition, provided the plants quickly recover from the move as they usually do, and there is no trouble from diseases or pests while the plants are in the glasshouse. This rich looking foliage will prove to be an asset in setting off the flowers, often increasing their market price.

CHAPTER EIGHTEEN

Growing in Pots

As POT PLANTS, chrysanthemums are available over a long period and can be had in bloom when other flowering pot plants are relatively scarce. Grown in this way, they are valuable plants for standing in the living-room, and the decorator will find many uses for them from the time they first appear on the market until the end of the chrysanthemum season. Now that year round production of chrysanthemums is being carried out, it may be that soon plants will always be available. The early flowering, mid-season and late varieties can all be used for pots, the chief difference in cultivation being the time of propagation.

It is, of course, quite usual to grow the later flowering varieties in the garden or field during the summer and then to lift them at the end of September for flowering under glass. This has proved satisfactory, although, of course, it cannot be expected that such treatment will produce the highest quality blooms. It is certainly an advantage to be able to lift chrysanthemums at all, and they can in some respects be regarded as a catch crop, following greenhouse tomatoes and being 'over' before the next crop is planted in the new year.

To have really first class blooms from later flowering varieties, it is really best to grow the plants in pots from the rooted cutting stage onwards. The usual procedure is to take the cuttings from the end of February, according to variety, and insert them in boxes or trays of sandy soil. When they are rooted, move them to 3 inch pots using a good, fairly rich compost. One, two or three cuttings can be put in each pot, according to the freedom with which the particular variety is likely to 'break' and the number of times it will be possible to stop the plants. Cuttings of the same size and vigour should be placed in the same pot, for ungraded cuttings will lead to eventual unsatisfactory growth.

Keep the pots in a cool temperature until the rooted cuttings are established, when they can be moved to cold frames from the beginning of April onwards. After a move to the 4½ or 5 inch pots, the plants are placed in the 8 or 10 inch size according to growth made. When risk of frosts is past, they are stood outside without cover, but in a place where they are not likely to be damaged or blown over by winds.

It is necessary not only to harden off the plants gradually so that they do not suffer from the lower temperatures, but their growth should not be hard, for if it is, it will mean stunted plants with few flowers. Although too much nitrogen in the compost can lead to soft, sappy growth, sometimes there is insufficient available. This is more likely to be the case when the John Innes composts are used, for the organic nitrogen supplied in the base dressing rapidly nitrifies under warm soil conditions, and in nitrate form, is continually leached in the course of watering. For this reason, it is advisable to feed with a nitrogen proprietary feed from time to time. Do this when the compost is already moist to avoid the possibility of damage by root scorching.

For the various pottings on, use a firm and roomy bench to ensure even potting. Finger pressure on the new compost down the sides of the larger pots, followed by two or three sharp taps with the bottom of the pot on the bench, usually works the soil in well. A blunt ended piece of wood can also be used, as a rammer, to work in the new soil around the sides of the pot.

The soil should always be finished off 2 or 3 inches from the top of the pot to allow for watering and top dressing as the season advances. At each move, the ball of soil should be about ½ inch below the surface of the new soil. While it is now common practice to grow plants in smaller size final pots than used to be the case, it is important to remember that with a smaller amount of soil in which to grow, regular feeding is necessary. Occasional light overhead sprinklings of water are helpful, especially in warm weather.

The outdoor standing ground is important and a cinder bed is ideal. It can be easily levelled and drainage is good. One drawback which has long troubled growers as far as the standing bed is concerned, is that weeds and grass are liable to grow up through and around the cinders. These may be of some value in keeping the pots cool, preventing water loss, but such weeds do present an untidy appearance, and if allowed to seed, other weeds spring up everywhere. What is worse, weeds often act as hosts to pests, which subsequently attack the plants. Instead of standing the pots on cinders or a similar base, it is better to stand them on black 150 gauge, polythene sheeting, spreading this, over the entire standing ground or in strips where the pots are to be placed. This prevents weeds from coming through. It is essential to see that the ground is firm and level so that water does not gather at the base of the pots. To avoid stagnant moisture, some growers place a thin layer of gravel over the polythene which allows the surplus water to escape or be soaked up. Any roots which work their way through the drainage hole into the gravel will easily come away when the plants are taken indoors.

Each plant will, of course, have a separate cane support which is driven into the pot while the plants are small. The plants are kept tied to the cane as growth develops. With regard to watering, this should be done as required, and the rule should be to give a thorough soaking and not very frequent sprinklings. The frequency of watering is largely influenced by weather conditions and some pots will need more water than others. While it may be quite sufficient to water once a week to begin with, later it may be necessary to give moisture at two-day intervals. Watch for the requirements of each pot so that there is no fear of waterlogging or sourness. Do not begin feeding too soon. On the other hand, do not wait until the plants are starved before helping them. Perhaps the best guide is to find out when the pots are full of roots. This can be done by carefully knocking out a plant to discover how big the root system is.

Some stopping will be needed, although the date is not so important as with plants for showing on a particular date. The early flowering varieties can be stopped in the same way as for plants growing in the open ground. The end of May or early June is a good time for the November flowering sorts, while the December varieties can be stopped twice, about the middle of April and again in mid-June. If any of the November flowering plants are particularly advanced in growth, they could be stopped first in April and then in early June. If, of course, some plants are more forward than others, it would prolong the flowering period. Unwanted side shoots must be constantly removed, tying regularly done and a watch kept for insect pests or possible diseases. The necessary precautions regarding these are the same as those mentioned in the separate chapters on the subjects.

The exact date for housing pot plants will depend on the season and also locality, for in open, cold districts they will need to be taken indoors earlier than in warm places. The normal time is from the end of September onwards.

Careful handling is needed, for every broken shoot means the loss of a flower. Some growers make a point of moving all plants when they are slightly on the dry side and therefore less brittle. Even when the plants appear to be quite clean, a good general spray will do good, or should mildew be in evidence on other plants in either the garden or greenhouse, a fungicide spray will be beneficial.

Each plant should be given room to stand quite clear of its neighbour so that all have air and light. This also makes it easy for watering and picking the flowers. Free ventilation is needed, for the plants must not become soft. Frost must, of course, be excluded from the house.

Liquid feeds are best from this time; indeed, it seems unlikely that solid fertilisers will break down at all. Do not continue to feed once the flower buds show colour. Unwanted side shoots and basal growths should be kept removed while they are small.

Numerous varieties of chrysanthemums have been grown with success in pots, some growers succeeding with certain sorts better than with others. Of the early flowering varieties, it is best to stick to the shorter growing kinds, but it is really the later flowering sorts that are so valuable for pot work. The following are all good:

White. Blanche du Poitou, mid-October; American Beauty, December; Marie Morin, November; Monument and its cream form, December; The Favourite, December.

Pink. Agnes Ford, December; May Wallace, November; Rose Poitevene, November.

Red. Baldock's Crimson, December; Red Favourite, December; Shirley Late Red, December; Balcombe Flame, Early November.

Yellow. Constance Baker, end-October; Yellow Fiona, November; Friendly Rival, December.

Singles, November flowering. Desert Chief, orange-amber; Desert Song, terra-cotta; Mason's Bronze, bright bronze; Molly Godfrey, pink.

Many of the dwarf pompons are excellent for pot work too.

Less common chrysanthemums which make excellent pot plants, especially where space is limited, include the Woolman's New Perpetuals, which form plants 6 to 12 inches in height and can be brought into bloom at any time of the year depending on the season of propagation. For instance, cuttings rooted in early January will produce blooms in early spring.

Not only so, since later crops of flowers will appear on subsequent growths, it is possible to use these same plants for bedding out later in the year.

The dainty single, daisy-like flowers of the Charm chrysanthemum are borne in great profusion and in a very wide range of colours. These blooms are light and dainty and make a welcome change from the more usual types. Seed is sown in January, the young plants being potted on until they reach the 8 inch size in which the low mounds of shoots, 18 to 24 inches across, are covered with flowers. Separate colours are now available including white, yellow, apricot, red and pink.

Then there are the dwarf Lilliputs and, of course, the popular dwarf pompons, such as Janté Wells, yellow; Cameo, white; Imp, crimson, and Trudie, pale pink.

None of these smaller growing types require stopping or disbudding. They look best when producing their blooms on free branching, bushy plants.

CHAPTER NINETEEN

Stopping and Timing Chrysanthemums

THERE ARE a number of words and terms used in connection with chrysanthemum growing which may sometimes seem a little puzzling. One of these is 'stopping'. The problems to solve in this matter would appear to be why, when and how should one stop any particular variety. But we may legitimately, if ungrammatically, ask, 'Stop the plants from what?'

The term stopping as applied to chrysanthemums simply implies the taking out of the growing tip of a plant to encourage it to 'break' or form a number of shoots from the leaf axils. Stopping is done with the finger and thumb, no fully developed leaves being taken off as a rule. Often the shoots would develop of their own accord, but the removal of the top of the plant causes them to grow more quickly, and usually to produce better and earlier blooms than if left to their own devices.

In order that we may be able to follow exactly what happens as a result of stopping a plant, there are a number of terms used by chrysanthemum growers which may need a little explanation, since often they are words or phrases which are used in a different setting to what is usually understood.

If a plant is allowed to grow on naturally it will form a bud at the top of the stem. This is known as the break bud. Almost always, it is surrounded by a number of vigorous growing side shoots which often grow more quickly than the central one. The break bud, if left, would very rarely produce a flower of any real value. The one possible exception to this is where very late cuttings have been taken and there is little time for a crop of side buds to form. The shoots which surround the terminal growth or break bud are known as lateral growths or breaks. If a plant is allowed to go unstopped and the break bud does develop, this is known as a natural break.

There are some varieties which are known to produce numerous shoots, and often, in these cases, the top of the shoot is removed before the laterals develop. Some growers refer to this as an anticipated natural break.

The shoots which develop from this or the natural break, are known as the first crown buds. These of course, are the first buds to appear at the tips of the flowering stems after a natural break. Sometimes more shoots appear than are needed, particularly when really large blooms are required.

The extra shoots can be removed and this is referred to as 'counting down'. Occasionally, with some varieties, the first crown buds are surrounded by other flower buds. It is then known as the terminal bud and no further upward growth will be made by that stem, so that the terminal bud is the latest bud that can be had on that variety.

Another rather obscure term sometimes employed is 'running on'. It is used when the first crown bud is surrounded by vegetative shoots. In this case, both the bud and the uppermost shoot on the stem are removed. The second shoot is allowed to produce a flower but all

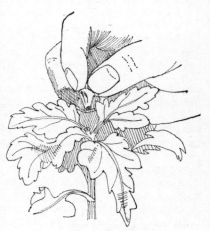

FIG. 5.—Removing the growing point, or 'stopping' a plant.

other lateral shoots on the stem are taken off. This procedure is sometimes adopted if the first crown bud develops too early or is accidentally damaged or broken, or if it happens to be on a very short stem.

Some varieties yield their best flowers from a second crown bud. These are produced not by 'running on' but by stopping twice, by a natural break and a stop. Each of the resultant shoots will make a natural break or is stopped, the flowers being 'taken' from the shoots that develop. Any and all additional shoots which appear should be removed while they are very small. This may be said to be another example of 'counting down'.

Some of the later varieties will produce good blooms on third crowns. This, of course, occurs when the second crowns are allowed to 'run on' with a further shoot. Where the aim is to produce blooms towards the end of December, some of the mid-season sorts are flowered on third crowns. It is rarely that such blooms are first class, but their lateness makes them valuable when used in the home or sent to market.

We must not imagine that by merely stopping plants we can produce the best quality flowers just when we want them. There is more in it than that. The health of the plant, the time the cuttings are taken and the general growing conditions all have an influence on the quality and time of the blooms.

It is obvious that if left untouched, chrysanthemum plants would produce quite a lot of flowers, in fact so many that they would be too small to be of use for either garden decoration or for cutting. This, of course, is why plants of the early flowering outdoor sorts are stopped while they are fairly small.

With these varieties, there is no need for an involved stopping plan to make the plants bloom out of season. It is the mid-season and late varieties on which the full stopping procedure can be carried out. It is when one is growing for exhibition or needs flowers on a particular date, that stopping and timing assume great importance. Experience has shown when it is necessary to stop certain varieties so that they flower at particular times. Much information on this matter can be had on reference to the catalogues of the specialist chrysanthemum growers or to the publications of the National Chrysanthemum Society. Even so, it is a very good plan to keep a note of the dates you stop certain varieties and of the exact date the flowers were in their prime. This will be a guide for future seasons and will indicate whether stopping is needed earlier or later for a particular purpose.

It will never be possible by any system of stopping to make an early flowering variety into a late, although the stopping of certain mid-season sorts will put back their flowering time.

Experience has shown that some really good varieties have flowers with a poor stem or a weak neck. Very often a plant which has blooms like this on the first crown can be put right by two stoppings, that is, by growing the bloom on the second crown bud. In addition, with some chrysanthemums which are naturally inclined to produce very few shoots, which is a great drawback if the aim is to produce plenty of cut flowers, a couple of stoppings leads to the production of the wanted laterals. It is also noticeable that flowers from the second crown bud are of better colour than those from a natural break or a first crown bud. On the other hand, it is not unknown for some varieties, particularly the whites and yellows, to be shaded with pink or yellow which certainly is not a consolation for stopping.

Then there are some varieties which are liable to produce flowers with too many petals to give a good bloom. Growing such sorts on the second crown bud will usually mean a reduction in petals and a better shaped flower. A further point is that some varieties which naturally produce thin petals can be improved by stopping. Against this, some blooms which are really good on the first bud prove disappointing on the second, and will give almost single flowers.

Stopping and timing are terms which are closely linked as far as chrysanthemum growing is concerned. In fact, apart from stopping plants in their early stages of growth to encourage lateral shoots to develop, the whole idea of stopping is to induce flowers to be at their best during a particular period – in many cases, where exhibitors are concerned – on a special day.

Fig. 6.—A disbudded plant with first crown buds secured.

Although it is impossible to generalise, it is useful to know that about seven weeks normally elapses between a stopping and the showing of a flower bud in the centre of the 'break growths' and there is a similar period between the appearance of the bud and the opening of the mature flower. This, however, must not be regarded as a fixed period. Some varieties may make their growths within say, six weeks, others may be slower and need eight or more weeks. Obviously weather and general conditions have a lot to do with the exact time.

Perhaps the safest way of making sure of blooms on a particular day is to grow sufficient plants to allow some to be stopped at intervals of six or seven days both before and after the normally calculated date. This should ensure tiptop flowers being available when specially required.

There is one other way of influencing the exact time of flowering, and that is the stage or time at which the shoots which develop round the bud are removed. If they are taken off as soon as they can be rubbed out, the flower bud will have greater opportunity to develop quickly. On the other hand, if left for a short time, or if there are a number of these side shoots or buds and they are only gradually removed, some being allowed to grow a little, flowering can be delayed for some days.

Feeding is dealt with in another chapter, but it can be used to control time of blooming, up to perhaps six or seven days. Nitrogen and phosphates have a great influence. The former is, of course, vital in the production of good coloured foliage which is always an asset to any flower. It should not be given, however, in the later stages of growth with the idea of hastening the appearance of the blooms. Feeding with a fertiliser having a high nitrogen content is, in fact, liable to delay blooming and is sometimes used for that purpose. If the flower buds are late or slow, apply a feed rich in phosphates and potash. Watering should also be reduced but not, of course, entirely withheld.

When stopping the early flowering varieties, it is wise to remember that whether they are the dwarf or the tall varieties, they invariably produce the best flowers on the first crown buds. It is wise to wait until the plants have produced the necessary number of side growths, and when these have formed, the growing tip from each one can be removed. It is unnecessary, in fact unwise, to take off any fully developed leaves. By stopping the growths early the flowers form on the lower shoots, and it is these that give the longest stems which are such an asset, particularly in the case of certain varieties which otherwise might be rather dumpy looking.

It is difficult if not impossible, to give a table of stopping dates for the early flowering varieties, but it must not be left too late otherwise there will be insufficient time for the plants to flower out of doors without protection. The second week in June should generally be regarded as the latest time, although there are one or two varieties which can be stopped at the beginning of the third week of that month.

After the earlies have been stopped they must be encouraged to make even, steady growth. Occasional overhead sprayings of clear water in the evenings during hot weather will be most helpful, but do not begin to feed until the plants are in full growth. It may not be necessary at all if they are growing in good compost, especially if the cuttings have come from a really strong stock. In fact, a good start makes all the difference between thoroughly satisfactory and indifferent results, and the grower should always get the best cuttings or plants that are available.

When we come to the pot grown chrysanthemum the stopping procedure becomes a little more involved. Although a lot of the mid-season varieties flower well on the first crown buds and the late sorts are usually given two stops, this is by no means the rule, and each variety should be treated individually. It is always helpful to observe (or find out from specialist growers if a new variety is being grown) whether the plant is a naturally tall or dwarf grower. Some of the former rarely produce side shoots low down on the stems, whereas many of the shorter growing kinds form laterals all along the stalks.

It is a great help if notes are made in regard to the varieties which are stopped, with dates of stopping and flowering, plus the general behaviour of the plants under this treatment. Such information will be invaluable in the next and future years. It never does to rely on memory or even to go by what one is told, for plants behave differently in one district from what they do in another. Such records will also show whether it is worth stopping particular varieties once or twice, and will also give guidance on how to stop in order to avoid thin petalled or over-full blooms.

Length of stem is always important, and here again it is experience that will provide the best guide as to the number of stops and the time to make them. As a rule, one may say the nearer the second stop is left to the second natural break, the shorter the stems will be. As far as 'running on' is concerned, it should be

22. Rayonnante or Spider Chrysanthemums in variety

23. *Chrysanthemum maximum* 'Moonlight'

24. *Below:* Annual Chrysanthemum, tricolor mixed

done as soon as the bud shows. This will result in both a good and a straight stem.

Much valuable information regarding stopping and timing will be found in the publications of The National Chrysanthemum Society, as well as all matters regarding the cultivation of this wonderful flower.

No one who joins the society can fail to obtain a tremendous amount of help. One is able to share the experiences of the leading amateur and professional growers, and is kept abreast of all the latest developments in the chrysanthemum world.

As a guide I have selected a number of the most popular varieties from several of the sections and give the time of rooting the cuttings with appropriate stopping dates, and the buds on which the flowers should be taken. Details of many other varieties will be found in the N.C.S. publications.

Obviously, if the rooting time is varied, this will have some influence on the stopping dates. The times given are for the southern half of the country and there will need to be some variation for the north and for Scotland. For instance, when in the south rooting dates are given as mid-January, it would need to be early January in the other areas, for whereas with many other garden operations, the colder the district the later the job must be done, with chrysanthemums it is the other way round.

STOPPING KEY FOR LARGE FLOWERED EXHIBITION INCURVED VARIETIES

Section 1 Exhibition Incurved (a) Large-flowered	Times of Rooting	Stopping Dates	Crown Bud
ANNIE CURRY	Mid-January	20th April – 25th June	2nd
AUDREY SHOESMITH	Mid-January	N.B.	1st
ENID WOOLMAN	Mid-January	20th April – 25th June	2nd
HILDA BIRCH	Mid-January	N.B.	1st
JACQUELINE WOOLMAN	End January	N.B.	1st
LILIAN SHOESMITH	End January	15th June	1st
MAGIC CIRCLE	End January	15th June	1st
MAXINE	Mid-January	20th April – 25th June	2nd
MECCA	Mid-January	N.B.	1st
ONDINE	End January	N.B.	1st

Section 1 Exhibition Incurved (a) Large-flowered	Times of Rooting	Stopping Dates	Crown Bud
ONWARD	March	N.B.	1st
VICTOR SHOESMITH	February	N.B.	1st

Section 1 Exhibition Incurved (b) Medium-flowered			
ANN RILEY	Early February	N.B.	1st
COON	Early February	N.B.	1st
J. H. GODDARD	Early February	N.B.	1st
MARY YULE	Mid-February	N.B.	1st
PINK CLOUD	Mid-February	N.B.	1st
PROGRESS	Mid-January	14th April N.B.	2nd
RITA SHOESMITH	Early February	N.B.	1st
RON SHOESMITH	Mid-January	N.B.	1st
VERA WOOLMAN	Mid-January	14th April N.B.	2nd
YELLOWSTONE	March	N.B.	1st

Section 2 Large Exhibition			
BETTY BARNES	Mid-January	15th May	1st
BIRMINGHAM	End January	N.B.	1st
CHARLES WOOLMAN	End December	7th May	1st
COSSACK	Mid-January	N.B.	1st
DUKE OF KENT	End December	20th May	1st
EDITH WOOLMAN	Early January	N.B.	1st
JAFFA	End January	30th May	1st
JAMES BRYANT	End November	6th March	1st
JESSIE HABGOOD	End December	10th May	1st
ORPHEUS	Mid-January	1st June	1st
PURPLE PRINCE	Early January	1st May	1st
RUBY WOOLMAN	Mid-January	25th May	1st
SHIRLEY AMBER	Mid-January	N.B.	1st
THOMAS W. POCKETT	Early January	N.B.	1st
VICKI WOOLMAN	Mid-January	25th May	1st

Section 3 Large Exhibition Incurving			
ALBERT BARNES	Early January	25th May	1st
ALBERT SHOESMITH	End December	N.B.	1st
CHRISTINE WOOLMAN	Early January	N.B.	1st
ELIZABETH EDNEY	Early January	N.B.	1st
GORDON HABGOOD	Early January	25th April	1st
SHIRLEY PRIMROSE	End December	15th March N.B.	2nd

Section 4 Medium Exhibition	Times of Rooting	Stopping Dates	Crown Bud
CONNIE MAYHEW	Mid-January	30th March N.B.	2nd
EDNA GREEN	Mid-January	N.B.	1st
MARY ALESWORTH	Mid-January	N.B.	1st
ODETTE	Mid-January	N.B.	1st
TALISMAN	Mid-January	N.B.	1st
WINN QUINN	Mid-January	N.B.	1st

The letters N.B. indicate natural break varieties. These, however, should be stopped if they have not made a natural break by the 15th June.

CHAPTER TWENTY

Exhibiting Chrysanthemums

THERE IS GREAT pleasure to be gained from growing really good chrysanthemums for garden display and for cutting for house decoration, or for giving to friends. It is perhaps part of human nature that one wishes to share with others the results of the care given to the plants over many months.

Experience shows that whether one grows half a dozen or a hundred plants, there is the constant desire to improve one's standards. From this stage there usually comes an interest in seeing what other gardeners have achieved, and before long there are visits to chrysanthemum shows and then participation in them.

It is unlikely that the value of prizes secured at exhibitions will cover the cost of producing the bloom, but monetary awards are not the chief concern of the true chrysanthemum exhibitor.

Records show that the first chrysanthemum society in this country was founded in 1846. From the information available, it seems evident that even in those far off days there was keen rivalry among enthusiasts of this flower, sometimes appropriately known as the Queen of the Autumn.

This original society from which has developed the National Chrysanthemum Society has grown steadily throughout the years, and by 1960 not only were there approaching 10,000 members and fellows but 1,400 affiliated societies. There must be many other societies not yet affiliated to the National body, and when one considers that in very many other 'general' societies there is quite a strong chrysanthemum section, it will be seen how keen has become the competition spirit. It is pleasing to see the friendly rivalry that exists, and that it is only on very, very rare occasions that there is any dissatisfaction with the awards made by qualified judges.

Like many other pursuits, the exhibiting of chrysanthemums is something which grows on one until it seems almost essential to match one's skill against that of other exhibitors. Perhaps it is because successful showing indicates the ability to grow properly, and in one sense exhibiting as the showing of what one can do and how one has mastered the growing techniques.

This, I think, is much more so in the case of chrysanthemums than with many other flowers.

At the same time, it is necessary for the exhibitor to know what is required on the show bench and upon what points the judges base their decisions. Anyone who intends to exhibit should study the show schedule before deciding which flowers to enter, for it is evident that if the regulations governing the show are ignored one cannot hope to meet with success. Even in small matters one can go astray, which is why the schedule must be read with care.

Entries for the various classes have to be submitted some time before the show date. Since there are so many sections of chrysanthemums it is important to enter the right classes, and when there is any doubt it is advisable to approach the Secretary so that no mistake is made.

If a class calls for a certain number of flowers, make sure that the number is correct. It is more than surprising how often an exhibitor seems unable to count! To the grower who has spent a long time tending his plants and has got his blooms into tiptop condition on show day, it can be more than annoying to see the words 'Not according to schedule' written across the card. This, of course, is a polite way of writing 'disqualified'. So often when this happens, it is due to a lack of studying the schedule, or of not contacting a show official.

Even if you think the schedule is wrong or could be improved or if you do not care for the officers of the society, the fact that you have entered the show classes binds you to the rules, if you are going to be among the winners.

At this point, it is as well to remind readers that it is always advisable to take more flowers to an exhibition than will be needed for the classes entered. So often one finds that some flowers which looked in tiptop form at home do not look quite so good at staging time. Blooms may become accidentally damaged in transit. It has been known, too, for filled vases to fall over in the course of staging, although this should not happen if normal precautions are taken when staging is being done.

Much is heard about the classification of chrysanthemums, and it is of course, necessary to get to know something about this matter if you intend showing blooms. In fact, if you are exhibiting at shows which are judged according to the National Chrysanthemum Society's classification, you must conform to the standards laid down. There is no doubt that this classification does help in defining the various types and sizes. It is not perfect but it does avoid a lot of confusion. Occasionally the National Chrysanthemum Society has had to move a variety from one class to another, but when this does happen, the flower is judged according to its classification at the time of the show.

Among the many benefits to be derived from joining the National Chrysanthemum Society is that, apart from all the other help you will gain, regular information is given on points regarding classification and show matters. I very much doubt whether the serious exhibitor can really afford not to join the National Society. The annual subscription is very modest, the 'service' is good and the literature received by members is interesting and detailed, and written by those who are actual growers of chrysanthemums and who therefore know the problems and in most cases at least, have discovered the answers too.

As far as detailed classification is concerned, for show purposes, the Floral Committee of the Society with the Royal Horticultural Society have drawn up the following table. This shows very clearly the sections or divisions recognised by the Society, and which apply where show classes are being judged in accordance with National Chrysanthemum Society rules:

CLASSIFICATION OF CHRYSANTHEMUMS

LATE-FLOWERING CHRYSANTHEMUMS, INDOOR VARIETIES

Section 1. *Exhibition Incurved*
    (a) Large flowered.
        Examples – Audrey Shoesmith, Victor Shoesmith, Yellow Marvel.
    (b) Medium flowered.
        Examples – Progress, Ron Shoesmith, Vera Woolman.

Section 2. *Large Exhibition*
    Examples – Charles Shoesmith, Duke of Kent, Majestic.

Section 3. *Large Exhibition Incurving*
Examples – Albert Shoesmith, Lilac Prince, Shirley Primrose.

Section 4. *Medium Exhibition*
Examples – Edward Page, Jean Ricardo, Winn Quinn.

Section 5. *Reflexed Decoratives*
(a) Large flowered.
Examples – Crimson Lake, Mary Selvey, Symbol.
(b) Medium flowered.
Examples – Marie Morin, My Lady, Princess Anne.

Section 6. *Incurving Decoratives*
(a) Large flowered.
Examples – Balcombe Perfection, Fred Shoesmith, Peace.
(b) Medium flowered.
Examples – Incurving Yellow Morin, Mayford Supreme, Woking Perfection.

Section 7. *Anemones*
(a) Large flowered.
Examples – Raymond Mounsey, Yellow Grace Land.
(b) Medium flowered.
Examples – Ceres, Elspeth, Heloise.
(c) Small flowered. i.e., Anemone Pompons.
Examples – Calliope, Mr. Astie.

Section 8. *Pompons*
(a) Large flowered.
Examples – Mdlle. Elise Dordan, Dresden China.
(b) Small flowered.
Examples – Baby, Ethel, Hilda Canning.

Section 9. *Singles*
Varieties with not more than five rows of ray florets.
(a) Large flowered.
Examples – Broadacre, Cleone, Peggy Stevens.
(b) Medium flowered.
Examples – Golden Seal, Mason's Bronze, Nancy Sherwood.
(c) Small flowered.
Examples – Godfrey's Gem, Market Gem.

Section 10. *Spidery, Plumed and Feathery*
> Examples – King of the Plumes, Mrs. Carter, Mrs. Filkins.

Section 11. *Any other Types*
> Example – Rayonnante.

OCTOBER FLOWERING CHRYSANTHEMUMS

NOTE: Varieties in Sections 16 and 17 are eligible for exhibition at both Early flowering and Late flowering Shows, as follows:

Section 16(a) for exhibition in Sections 21(a) or 5(a).
Section 16(b) for exhibition in Sections 21(b) or 5(b).
Section 17(a) for exhibition in Sections 22(a), 20(a), 6(a) or 1(a).
Section 17(b) for exhibition in Sections 22(b), 20(b), 6(b) or 1(b).

Section 16. *Reflexed*
> (a) Large flowered.
> Examples – Chairman, Leader, Perfection.
> (b) Medium flowered.
> Example – Yellow Gown.

Section 17. *Incurving*
> (a) Large flowered.
> Examples – Maestro, Marie Brunton, Susan Alesworth.
> (b) Medium flowered.
> Examples – Dorothy Wilson, Isabel.

EARLY-FLOWERING CHRYSANTHEMUMS, OUTDOOR VARIETIES

Definition of an Early-Flowering Chrysanthemum:

'An Early-Flowering Chrysanthemum is a variety which blooms in a normal season in the open ground before October 1st without any protection whatsoever.'

This definition does not debar exhibitors from protecting blooms from weather damage.

Section 20. *Incurved*
> (a) Large flowered.
> Examples – Ermine, John Woolman.
> (b) Medium flowered.
> Examples – Enid Walters, Globemaster, Jacqueline, Verinette.
> (c) Small flowered.
> Example – Moonstone.

Section 21. *Reflexed*
  (a) Large flowered.
      Examples – Dorothea, Kathleen Doward, Peter Shoesmith.
  (b) Medium flowered.
      Examples – Brenda Talbot, Brumas, J. R. Johnson, Regalia.
  (c) Small flowered.
      Examples – Sparkler, Wendy.

Section 22. *Incurving*
  (a) Large flowered.
      Examples – Charles Horwood, Evelyn Bush, Harry James, Westfield Bronze.
  (b) Medium flowered.
      Examples – Delightful, Silver Dollar.

Section 23. *Singles*
  (a) Large flowered.
      Examples – Daphne, Major Robertson.
  (b) Medium flowered.
      Examples – Caradoc, Doreen Woolman, Nectar.

Section 24. *Pompons*
  True Poms. The blooms of these varieties, when fully open, form a perfect ball of compact hard florets.
      Examples – Cameo, Fairie, Poppet.
  Semi-Poms. The blooms of these varieties, when fully open, form a cone of compact hard florets, with a flat base.
      Examples – Bright Eye, Denise, Tiptoe.

Section 25. *Any other Types* (including Koreans and Charms).
      Examples – Catena, Premiere.

Having made sure that the blooms we have are the correct ones for the classes entered, the next thing is to see that the flowers are cut at the right time and in the proper manner. It is a great pity to grow the plants well and then to treat them indifferently. It is always best to cut them in the early morning making sure to give the roots a thorough soaking the night before. The stems, cut as long as possible, should be plunged in deep water keeping them there and in cool surroundings, for some hours. The lower leaves should be removed, for not only do they take up water which might be needed by the stems, but they are liable to become messy and to foul the water. Some varieties take up water much better than others and it will be found most helpful to crush the ends of woody stemmed sorts to ensure that sufficient moisture is taken up for the proper support of the flowers. Alternatively, the bottom of the stem can be split for an inch or two.

Anyone who has grown chrysanthemums will know that they actually improve after being in water for some hours. Some exhibitors keep the stems plunged in deep water for twenty-four hours – often more. They should be stood in a draught free situation, preferably in a shaded position and certainly out of full light.

Particularly with the early flowering varieties, it is an asset that the blooms can be cut so long before the show, for this means that the risk of weather damage a few hours before showing time can be prevented.

Always avoid laying the flowers on the ground or on any other flat surface. If this is done, some of the florets are bound to be crushed and the petals likely to become soiled or marked.

The exhibitor should aim at selecting blooms that are uniform in size and colour. It is very noticeable that the colour of a variety can vary quite a lot with age. Blooms which have been gathered at different times will often appear to be a slightly different shade. It is, therefore, an advantage to pick the blooms for a particular class at the same time.

While fully developed flowers in prime conditions are, of course, the best ones to stage, it is better to show rather younger blooms which have not reached their peak than those which are past their best and are looking 'tired'.

It is essential, if blooms are to be among the prizewinners, to remove all damaged petals or florets. This means that each flower must be carefully examined for blemishes. Sometimes there is very slight insect damage, or individual petals may be marked in transit or when the blooms are being unpacked. This is where a pair of tweezers comes in handy, for they can be used to remove individual florets and also those at the back of the blooms.

The judge will look there, too, to see whether there are old florets. If there are, it will lower the points value of the bloom.

Do not attempt to improve the flowers while the petals are wet but wait until they are quite dry before the cleaning commences. Particular care is needed with the white or light coloured sorts which seem to spot more freely, and for that reason may need extra attention. Make sure, too, that the foliage is clean and not showing signs of mildew or of leaf miner damage.

One can often find minor blemishes when the blooms are being staged. This is why it is advisable to arrive at the exhibition in plenty of time to stage the blooms. Hurried work will never be satisfactory, and when the staging of the exhibit is done calmly, nothing is likely to be overlooked. Also, the fact that near-by competitors may have larger blooms than yours will not unduly disturb or distress. The largest are not necessarily the best.

The following is the points system on which chrysanthemums are often judged and it is quoted from the Horticultural Show Hand Book by permission of the Royal Horticultural Society.

CHRYSANTHEMUMS, SECTION I – EXHIBITION INCURVED

Meritorious. A bloom which is compact and globular or nearly so. Florets which are broad, smooth, rounded at the tips, of sufficient length to form a graceful curve, closely and regularly arranged, firm, fresh (including the outer ones) and of a clear decisive colour.

Defective. A bloom which is loose, flat, has a hollow centre, or is irregular in outline. Florets which are narrow, pointed, loosely, or irregularly arranged, soft, lacking freshness or of a dull colour.

Note: No cups or rings are permissible, but the stem may be supported.

Form	7 points
Size	3 ,,
Freshness	7 ,,
Colour	3 ,,
	20 ,,

CHRYSANTHEMUMS, SECTION II – LARGE EXHIBITION (formerly known as Incurving Japanese)

Meritorious. A bloom which is globular or nearly so, with a full centre. Florets which are broad, incurved (either closely and regularly or loosely and irregularly), fresh to the tips and of a bright colour.

Defective. A bloom which lacks depth and is not globular, or has a hollow centre. Florets which are narrow not incurved, have stale tips or are of dull colour.

Note: Cups or wires may be used to support the blooms, but they must not exceed 3 in. in diameter.

For scale of points, see Section I.

CHRYSANTHEMUMS, SECTION IV – MEDIUM EXHIBITION

Meritorious. As in Sections II and III.
Defective. As in Sections II and III.

Form .	.	.	.	.	.	.	7 points
Size .	.	.	.	.	.	.	3 ,,
Freshness	.	.	.	.	.	.	7 ,,
Colour	.	.	.	.	.	.	3 ,,
Foliage	.	.	.	.	.	.	5 ,,
							25 ,,

CHRYSANTHEMUMS, SECTION V – REFLEXED DECORATIVES

Meritorious. Blooms which are broad and deep, and have full centres. Florets of good substance, bright in colour and fresh to the tips. In fully reflexing types, florets which reflex gracefully and overlap one another perfectly. In semi-reflexing types, a pleasing contrast in colour between the outer reflexing and the inner incurving florets. In types with quilled, sharply pointed florets which stand out stiffly; freshness to the tips is of particular importance.

Defective. Blooms which are narrow, or shallow, or which lack full centres or have 'daisy eyes', i.e. visible disk-florets. Florets which are of poor substance, stale, drooping, dull in colour ragged or misplaced.

Form .	.	.	.	.	.	.	7 points
Size .	.	.	.	.	.	.	3 ,,
Freshness	.	.	.	.	.	.	7 ,,
Colour	.	.	.	.	.	.	3 ,,
Foliage	.	.	.	.	.	.	5 ,,
							25 ,,

CHRYSANTHEMUMS, SECTION VI – INCURVING DECORATIVES

Meritorious. Blooms which are globular in outline, with breadth and depth approximately equal. Florets which are broad, incurving (either closely and regularly or loosely and irregularly) of good substance, fresh to the tips and of a bright colour.

Defective. Blooms which are too broad for their depth and not globular in outline or have hollow centres. Florets which are narrow, or which are not all incurving, or are of poor substance, or are of dull colour.

For scale of points see Section V.

CHRYSANTHEMUMS, SECTION VII – ANEMONE FLOWERED

Meritorious. Blooms which have fresh, deep, symmetrical 'cushions' (i.e. disks) of even size and a bright colour. Ray florets which are fresh to the tips and of a bright colour, but they may be either broad to the tips, flat and of equal length, or pointed and of uneven size.

Defective. Blooms with cushions which are stale, shallow, malformed, of uneven size or dull in colour. Ray florets which are drooping, or not fresh to the tips, or are of a dull colour.

For scale of points, see Section V.

CHRYSANTHEMUMS, SECTION VIII – POMPONS

Meritorious. Flowers which are symmetrical, with full centres, of uniform size and a bright colour.

Defective. Blooms which are unsymmetrical, lack full centres, are of uneven size or of a dull colour.

For scale of points, see Section V.

CHRYSANTHEMUMS, SECTION IX – SINGLE FLOWERED

Meritorious. Flowers borne at right angles to the stems. Ray florets which are broad, flat, of good substance, fresh to the tips and of a bright colour. Disk florets which are fresh bright and regular.

Defective. Flowers which are not borne at right angles to the stems. Ray florets which are in excess of five rows, or are narrow, incurving or not flat, or are of poor substance, drooping stale or of a dull colour. Disk florets which are old, of a dull colour or irregular.

For scale of points, see Section V.

CHRYSANTHEMUMS, SECTION XVI – OCTOBER FLOWERING REFLEXED VARIETIES

As in Section V.

CHRYSANTHEMUMS, SECTION XVII – OCTOBER FLOWERING INCURVING VARIETIES

As in Section VI.

CHRYSANTHEMUMS, SECTION XVIII – LARGER OCTOBER FLOWERING VARIETIES

As in Sections V and VI.

CHRYSANTHEMUMS, SECTION XX – OUTDOOR INCURVED VARIETIES

Meritorious. As in Section I.
Defective. As in Section I.
For scale of points, see Section V.

CHRYSANTHEMUMS, SECTION XXI – OUTDOOR REFLEXED VARIETIES

As in Section V.

CHRYSANTHEMUMS, SECTION XXII – OUTDOOR INCURVING VARIETIES

As in Section VI.

CHRYSANTHEMUMS, SECTION XXIII – OUTDOOR SINGLE VARIETIES

As in Section IX.

CHRYSANTHEMUMS, SECTION XXIV – OUTDOOR POMPON VARIETIES
As in Section VIII.

CHRYSANTHEMUMS, SPECIMEN PLANTS IN POTS

Meritorious. A symmetrical plant 'facing all round', with a single main stem for not less than 1 in. between the soil and the first branch or break. Blooms numerous and of high quality. Foliage ample, clean and healthy. Stems which have been bent gradually from near their bases. Supports and ties inconspicuous.

Defective. A plant which is not symmetrical, or which faces only one way, or has more than one main stem immediately above the soil. Blooms which are not sufficiently numerous for the size of the plant or are lacking in quality. Stems which have been bent abruptly. Supports or ties which are obtrusive, or ties which are too near the blooms.

Number, quality and freshness of the blooms	10 points
Foliage	4 ,,
Training	6 ,,
	20 ,,

VASES, BOWLS OR BASKETS ARRANGED FOR EFFECT

It is difficult to lay down hard and fast rules for the judging of classes of this nature as the 'effect' must necessarily vary according to the particular taste of the individual.

Standard of Quality. The following general principles to be observed are given as a guide. The exhibit should have lightness and a pleasing arrangement of Chrysanthemum blooms, in association (at the option of the exhibitor) with fern, natural foliage, berries or grasses, without overcrowding. There should be either uniformity of colour or harmonious blending of colours. The blooms should be of good quality, fresh and not bruised or damaged.

Lightness and artistic arrangement	35 points
Harmony of colours or uniformity of colour	25 ,,
Quality and freshness of blooms and foliage	35 ,,
Container	5 ,,
	100 ,,

Common Faults. Overcrowding and heaviness of effect. Faded blooms. Discord of colours. Gaps and lack of symmetry.

CHAPTER TWENTY-ONE

Year Round Production

ALTHOUGH the production of chrysanthemums throughout the year has been practised in the United States for quite a long time, it is only fairly recently that it has been done on any great scale in this country.

There are many people who shrink from the idea of having chrysanthemums available throughout the year and this is something which will have to be overcome if this method of production is to increase. If, of course, florists and the public want and use the flowers in the spring and summer as well as the normal months, more will be grown.

No one can deny that chrysanthemums are of special value because of their long lasting qualities, their wide colour range and the many uses to which they can be put.

All the year round production is not something which can be taken on lightly, for it involves care at all stages. Any failure to provide the right condition at any time during growth is bound to have an adverse effect upon results. Then there is the extra expense involved in providing the necessary equipment for year round cropping.

Light has a far greater effect on the development of chrysanthemums than most of us realise. Plants have been classified by scientists as 'long day', 'short day' and 'indifferent' groups, according to their reaction to the length of daylight.

We all know that the varieties which normally flower in this country during November and December are short day plants and are those which produce leaves and stems when the days are long, and do not begin to develop flower buds until the hours of daylight shorten. Flowering can be delayed if required, by introducing artificial light into the greenhouse. This does not, as some

143

imagine, give the plants more time in which to grow each day but actually retards the development of the flower buds. Bud initiation takes place when there are less than fourteen hours of daylight. To replace natural light it is possible to fix up 75 watt electric bulbs, 6 feet apart, and about 3 feet above the plant, or if 40 watt bulbs are used, they should be spaced 4 feet apart and $2\frac{1}{2}$ feet higher than the plants. The growth of plants can also be controlled by shortening the days, and for this, the plants are covered for some hours with black plastic or polythene. Such covering must be well above the plants so that there is no contact, and it is left in position for the necessary number of hours and then removed.

Temperature is also important and has a great influence in determining plant responses, for it affects water and nutrient absorption, respiration, transpiration and other factors which control growth. It is essential to maintain a night temperature of 60 degrees F.

The response which certain varieties give in regard to flowering according to the amount of light is known as Photoperiodism.

As yet, all the year production is mostly being carried out by commercial growers, and since it is important to start with the right stock, it is often the wisest plan to obtain cuttings or young plants from specialist firms who will be able to supply on and for, specific dates.

For those who wish to take their own cuttings, they can be obtained from selected stock plants. Varieties are chosen according to the length of time they take to grow; for suitability in the long days of summer, or the short days of winter. They must also be chosen for the colour most suited to the season in which they will flower.

Cuttings are inserted in gritty soil which professional growers usually sterilise. Rooting is achieved in twelve to fourteen days in a temperature of 60 degrees F. which is maintained until the bud initiation stage.

The cuttings are pinched off periodically from the selected stools to an equal length of about 3 inches. As one lot of cuttings is taken, the next batch will be stimulated into growth. In the winter months, the production of cuttings from the stock plants slows down to about a third or so of summer production.

Shading and lighting varies with the time of year. From April to August, lamps are unnecessary; during the winter months no shading is required. In the spring, black polythene is used for

25. 'Weldmesh', galvanised wire supports in the greenhouse

26. 'Weldmesh', wire square supports outdoors

27. Showing effect of flower distortion virus on 'Annie Curry'

28. Leaf attacked by Chrysanthemum mildew

29. Adult leaf miner seen on Chrysanthemum leaf

30. Showing typical injury done by leaf miner

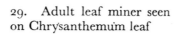

shading. Peat and manure are always required when the green-house beds are being prepared and liquid feeding can be applied as the plants develop.

Wires and cross strings are used to support the plants and are raised as growth develops.

Quick growth is encouraged by supplying plenty of water and keeping the beds really moist. As the buds are being initiated, watering is lessened to avoid the possibility of weak necks but extra moisture is applied again once the buds break open. At this stage, too, the temperature is slightly and gradually reduced to improve the quality of the blooms.

Cleanliness is of vital importance at all stages, and it is advisable to spray the young plants at fortnightly intervals, with a good insecticide. This should be changed from time to time to prevent the build up of a resistant strain of aphids.

If temperature and ventilation are properly managed there should be no trouble from mildew, although an occasional spraying with a good fungicide will prove beneficial.

In the U.S.A., year round pot production is quite important and has made it possible for good plants to be available for Mothers' Day and Easter, as well as at all other times of the year. Tall varieties which are usually grown for cut flower purposes need fairly drastic treatment to reduce their height in pots and are usually pinched one week after short day treatment commences. This is known as a delayed pinch, and means the removal of the terminal bud and often the first two lateral buds initiated by the preceding week of short day treatments.

Since the breaks resulting from the pinch contain buds already initiated, the flowering is not delayed for any significant period.

For pot plants it is important for the compost to contain a good quantity of organic matter such as peat or rotted manure. This will improve water holding capacity and provide good general root condition.

It is customary to refer to varieties being grown on the year round system, as 9, 10, 12 or 13 week varieties. This is primarily a term used in connection with controlled flowering and implies the number of weeks of short days needed to make a variety flower. For example, a 9 week variety is one which will respond or flower 9 weeks after 'short days' are started. Starting short days is accomplished in summer by using black cloth or black polythene; in winter it means discontinuing lights at night.

Generally speaking 8 or 9 week varieties will be the early

flowering garden sorts, the 10 and 11 week ones are November blooming, the 12 to 15 kinds, those which flower from mid-December onwards.

As examples, Yellow Monument is in the 9 week response group, Fred Shoesmith and Shirley Late Red in the 11 week group.

The following table gives a clear picture of how the dates and flowering periods work out:

Planting Date	Start short days	Bloom	Weeks to Crop	Response Group
5/1	16/2	27/4	16	10
19/1	23/2	4/5	15	10
2/2	2/3	11/5	14	10
16/2	9/3	18/5	13	10
23/2	16/3	25/5	13	10
2/3	23/3	1/6	13	10
12/3	2/4	11/6	13	10
22/3	12/4	21/6	13	10
1/4	22/4	1/7	13	10
11/4	2/5	11/7	13	10
21/4	12/5	21/7	13	10
1/5	22/5	31/7	13	10

Planting Date	Start short days	Bloom	Weeks to Crop	Response Group
20/8	24/9	10/12	16	11
2/9	23/9	23/12	16	13
5/9	26/9	2/1	17	14
8/9	6/10	12/1	18	14
11/9	16/10	22/1	19	14
21/9	26/10	1/2	19	14
1/10	5/11	11/2	19	14
11/10	22/11	21/2	19	13
21/10	2/12	3/3	19	13
7/11	26/12	13/3	18	11
17/11	5/1	23/3	18	11
27/11	15/1	2/4	17	10

It is possible to produce three crops of blooms from the same bed in the course of a year. This could be done on the following lines:

	Plant	Light	Shade	In flower	Response group
First crop	May 25	—	13 June to bud colour	August 15	9
Second crop	Sept. 2	Sept. 2 – Oct. 2		December 18	11

	Plant	Light	Shade	In flower	Response group
Third crop	Jan. 11	Jan 11 – Feb. 19	20 March to bud colour	May 8	11

Full information on this system of cultivation is to be found in *Chrysanthemums All the Year Round* by Searle and Machin published by Blandford Press Ltd., 16 West Central Street, London W.C.1.

CHAPTER TWENTY-TWO

Chrysanthemums for House Decoration

THERE ARE FEW, if any, flowers which have such long lasting qualities as the chrysanthemum, this is why it is so valued as cut blooms. Although the stems are firm and erect growing, they are nevertheless easy to arrange, either when used alone or with other flowers, foliage and berried sprays. Apart from the early flowering and the mid-season and late decorative sorts, the Koreans, singles, anemone-centred and pompons and spidery Rayonnante varieties are all easy to arrange. The spray types are also excellent, and as necessary, the stems can be separated, otherwise the sprays may appear too 'bunchy' and heavy.

There need be no waste with chrysanthemums, for any flowers which have to be taken off or are broken from the main stems can be tucked in low down in the arrangement.

Although all the year round chrysanthemums now seem to be more than a possibility, for house decoration the flowers really come into their own after the summer blooming subjects have passed over. Although, as already stated, the chrysanthemum is so long lasting, there are occasions when the blooms seem to flag after being cut for a short while. There are two possible causes, either the plants have been forced, making the petals soft, leading to early wilting, or the stems are unable to take up water. While it is really best to cut the stems from the plant, leaving a sloping, rather than a straight surface, some of the stems are hard, and it is, therefore, a good plan to bruise or split the base of the stems, making it easy for water to be taken up. The lower leaves should be removed, for if left they are likely to foul the water and shorten the life of the flowers. Sometimes certain crystals or powders are used in the supposition that they lengthen the life of the blooms. Most of us have heard the assertion that if an aspirin tablet or a copper coin is placed in the container the flowers will last longer. I do not think that there is any real substantiation for such beliefs, and perhaps the best way of ensuring long life is to give the flowers a long drink in water before using them.

Then there is the question of the changing of the water used for the containers. Some floral decorators change the water daily, others believe in just topping up the vases as necessary. While bright sunlight shining directly on the plants is undesirable, cut blooms do like plenty of light and air. In continued dull light they are liable to lose their true colouring. Then, of course, the flowers should not be kept in a draught or be left in a warm room all night.

There is no limit to the type of containers which can be used; in fact, during recent years all sorts of pots, pans and vases have been employed with great effectiveness. It is often possible to obtain suitable receptacles from antique shops. For exhibition purposes the container must suit the arrangement being made, or the exhibit will be down pointed.

The arrangement will gain if the flowers are picked at varying stages of growth, so that buds and blooms are in different stages of development. Some will be in fairly tight bud, others just open, and yet others more fully open, but not, of course, past their best.

Marked or damaged petals should be removed, as should tired, limp looking foliage. If arranging for the pleasure of having the flowers in the house, one need not be so particular as to the final effect. Wire netting is needed to push into the vases before the flowers are inserted. The finer the mesh, the thinner must be the stalks. There are, of course, various holders available nowadays, some having a metal base from which arise wire stubs on which the stalks are impaled to keep them in position. Other holders have holes into which the stems are inserted, but the wire netting method is very suitable for keeping the blooms in the position. Flora-Pak is also very valuable for holding flowers in place.

It is best to keep in mind the final effect intended as one is building up the decoration. It is a great help if the outline is worked out so that it can be filled in to present a balanced effect. Foliage and berries are often very helpful, but do not overdo these and never overcrowd a vase. There is much to be learned from the Japanese in the way of building up a light, dainty arrangement. Avoid gaps and, excepting with a 'facing' display, view the arrangement from all sides and make sure that there is a focal point which can make or mar the whole creation.

As a rule, the lighter shades should be worked into the outline and the darker colours kept for filling in. At times when flowers are scarce, quite a lot can be done with even a half dozen blooms; in fact, in some of the modern line arrangements, as seen at flower shows, really interesting and pleasing displays have been created with five or six blooms and various types of foliage. As far as exhibiting is concerned, one must be guided by what the schedule says regarding the use of leaves or berries. For home decoration, the suitable material available is extremely wide.

Foliage should be chosen which will give more colour to the display either by blending with the blooms or by creating a pleasing contrast.

Kale and beetroot leaves are most useful for associating with chrysanthemums. Various berries, too, can be employed. To prevent berries falling prematurely, brush them over with glue or varnish, especially near the stem bases.

Then there are various grasses, bullrushes and even dock seed heads. These will give height to many designs. The maroon atriplex or mountain spinach used with pink chrysanthemums and a sprig or two of pernettya berries, mauve for preference, look superb, especially if one or two beetroot leaves are used at the base.

The maroon foliage of *Prunus pissardii* fits in well with deep pink flowers as do sprays of berberis foliage. *Asparagus plumosus* and *sprengeri* are useful where trails of foliage are needed, while there is use for the leaves of magnolia and the handsome *Begonia Rex*. The pointed foliage of gladioli can also prove more than useful. Leaves of copper beech worked in with salmon-pink chrysanthemums, grey foliage with the pale pink or white blooms, or red tinted leaves with autumn tonings, and red or white berries with similar coloured flowers are all possibilities.

Chrysanthemums are showy and attractive, bringing life to any room without in any way, being formal looking.

CHAPTER TWENTY-THREE

Raising new Chrysanthemums

FROM SEED

Although as we shall presently see, new varieties sometimes originate as sports from established sorts, many really worthwhile varieties are raised from seed. A large number of garden plants breed true to type from seed when care has been taken to see that they are self-pollinated. The chrysanthemum, however, produces a range of seedlings differing very widely in height, colour, shape and general characteristics.

This means that even when two chrysanthemums having the desired qualities are crossed, the resultant seedlings are not likely to combine the good points of both parents. Sometimes from a batch of seedlings it is possible to select one which shows promise and is worth growing on and propagating.

As a rule, hybridising is best left to the professional growers, although it can be an interesting pastime for the amateur as long as he is prepared for disappointments. Often, one may raise hundreds of seedlings without finding one of real interest.

Before considering the actual job of pollinating, it is necessary to know something of the flower with which we are dealing. The chrysanthemum belongs to the genus *compositae*, and the flower, as we know it, is actually a cluster of flowers, growing closely together to form one head. It is really more correct to use the word flowers or florets to describe the small individuals that make up the bloom. The bloom is the complete flower head.

The centre or eye of the bloom consists of disk florets, the anthers in these being the male or pollen bearing structures. When these are 'ripe' the pollen is distributed, which accounts for the yellow appearance in the centre of the bloom. The petals are really the ray florets and consist of the lengthened petal enclosing the ovary. There are no male organs in these florets.

As with other subjects, when a flower is fertilised by its own pollen it is said to be self-pollinated. When the pollen is carried from one flower to another by insects or wind, this is cross-pollination.

Because of the make up of a chrysanthemum bloom, only the ray florets are used for the receiving of the hybridising pollen. The actual pollen grains settle on the stigmas of the florets, which are sticky, and having done so, they each send out a tiny tube-like growth into the ovary, to fuse with the female germ cell. Normally this results in seed formation.

To prevent self-pollination before a cross is made, the disc florets of the double varieties should be very carefully removed with tweezers. To make this easy, the ray florets are cut back, bit by bit, until the green tip of the pistil is seen, which will be just before the ray florets reach their full size. After the cutting, the stigmas will continue to grow until they can easily be seen beyond the cut edge, where, of course, they may be fertilised by the selected pollen.

With the singles and the anemone-centred varieties, the whole of the centre or eye is cut back in order to remove the anthers, the ray florets being used for crossing. Unless the anthers or pollen bearers are removed, one cannot be sure that self fertilisation has not taken place.

It will readily be realised that although one may pollinate or place the pollen on the stigma, fertilisation does not occur until the pollen grain grows and enters the embryo seed in the ovary.

Sometimes the selected parent flowers are not ready for pollination at the same time. Fortunately, pollen will keep if stored in sterilised test tubes and placed in a refrigerator and kept in a temperature around 38 to 40 degrees F.

The actual pollinating is done with a tiny, fine camel hair brush, a flattened pin or even the point of a knife. I know of some growers who use a lightly sharpened matchstick for the job, and it is easy to use a fresh one for each cross. It is usual and I think best, to pollinate as many florets in each head as there is pollen available.

Records of all crosses made should be retained, for they are most useful for future reference. The pollinated head should be kept dry and in the light, and, of course, protected from damage by insects. Within a couple of days the stigmas will shrivel, and as the seed begins to develop, the plants should be given less water, as this encourages the ripening of the seed.

Some raisers cut the blooms for pollinating and stand them in water, which seems quite satisfactory, one advantage being that there is less, if any, possibility of the head 'damping' as sometimes occurs with the growing plants.

The heads must be quite dry before they are considered ripe. This means that there should be no trace of greenness when the florets are moved. It usually takes from six to eight weeks for seed to develop and ripen, and when they are ready, the 'head' will fall to pieces when moved. Before this happens, it should be enclosed in a bag so that no seed is lost. Label each bag and store in a dry place until required for sowing.

Early February is the best time for sowing, which should be done in pots of sandy compost to which some peat has been added. Keep in a temperature of 60 degrees F., and cover the pots with glass to prevent evaporation. When the seedlings can be handled, move them to small pots giving bigger receptacles according to growth. Subsequently, treat the plants in the normal way in regard to supporting and feeding. Keep suckers cut but do not pull them out. Then comes the period of waiting for flowers, when it will be seen if one has raised anything which promises to be worth propagating.

The hybridising of chrysanthemums is a fascinating pleasure, but there is no key to the production of particular colours, so that we cannot say that by crossing a white with a red variety that we shall raise a pink flowering sort.

FROM SPORTS

The modern chrysanthemum is the result of very many years of cross breeding and of inbreeding, so that we ought not to be surprised that there is a certain amount of instability of varieties. It is this fact that accounts for the appearance of so many mutations or 'sports' as they are more often said to be.

A sport is a distinct change which sometimes occurs in an established variety. This may be a change of colour, form or shape of the flower, the habit or vigour of growth, or in the normal date of blooming.

A plant may have remained fixed and true in every way for many years and then suddenly 'sport'. What is particularly interesting is that sometimes a particular variety will sport in different parts of the country in the same season. This means that if a good mutation appears it is necessary to ascertain whether it is already known – and perhaps named.

Sporting does occur in many other plants, but in the chrysanthemum this happening is a fruitful source of obtaining really good new named varieties. Many sports, however, are worthless and not nearly so good as the parent plant. On the other hand, most valuable new varieties have been produced in this way.

The varieties, Sweetheart, Una, H. E. Trueman, The Favourite, as well as others, have produced a whole series of different coloured sports which are sufficiently good enough to be grown and offered by specialist firms as separate varieties. There are others, which, while retaining their colour, have given sports of different habit, such as reflexing instead of incurving petals.

Most growers will have had sports in which only some of the petals are a different colour or shape, or just half the flower may be affected. If it is thought that there are possibilities with such happenings, one has to exercise patience by waiting for a year or two to see if complete flowers of the new type are produced. This, of course, means the propagating of stem cuttings from the sporting stems.

Even when a 'whole' flower develops, it is still necessary to make sure that the new colour or habit is fixed. This is done by growing basal cuttings from the sport in the same way as with fixed varieties. Young plants raised in this way for a couple of years, will prove whether the new characteristics are fixed.

Since it is usually only one stem of a plant which produces a sport, it is necessary to encourage this stem to throw out side shoots for the supplying of cuttings. This can be done by cutting all other stems back to soil level. Although the actual growing of the new cuttings is the same as with established varieties, the process of obtaining the new growth is different. Cut off the flower head. Then water the pot well and lay it on its side so that the stem is resting on soil which has been placed in a seed tray or something similar. Cover the stem with an inch of compost and give a light watering. If bottom heat is available, say about 50 degrees F., new shoots will develop in the usual way and can be taken as ordinary cuttings, being boxed or potted up.

Unfortunately, many sports are worthless and quite inferior to the plant from which they spring. Sometimes, too, they revert to the parent either wholly or in part. It is, therefore, most necessary for the grower to be quite satisfied that the sport is fixed, otherwise the stock must be discarded. This means, of course, watching the performance of the sports very closely for three years or so.

In order to have a sport confirmed and named as a new variety, the grower should apply to the Secretary of the National Chrysanthemum Society for a form to complete for the Floral Committee. Then arrangements are made for specimens of the new variety and usually a sample of the parent plant, to be sent for inspection.

As far as naming is concerned, the new plant would be registered in the raiser's name, but the Society now recommend that sports should bear part of the name of their parent. An example of this is seen in the sports which have come from Annie Curry. We now have Yellow Curry, Buff Curry, Pink Curry. Apart from showing their origin, such names do give an indication of the treatment required, since it is the same as that needed by the parent plant.

The actual cause of sporting has long been under investigation, and scientists believe that it is due to some change in the number of chromosomes in the outer layers of the cells of the plants.

CHAPTER TWENTY-FOUR

Less common Chrysanthemums

EVERY YEAR new varieties of chrysanthemums are introduced by both professional and amateur growers. Although because of competition, if for no other reason, new introductions have to be good, it is a fact that some of the newer sorts show no advance on varieties which have been in cultivation for some years. There are, of course, also a few new varieties brought to notice each year, which are a definite improvement in form, colour or size.

Not only is there a regular increase in the number of actual varieties, but in recent years there have been introduced a few entirely new sections. These have usually been the result of intensive breeding work by specialist growers.

LILLIPUTS

One noteworthy new type is that known as the Lilliput race. This was evolved by the firm of H. Woolman Ltd., of Shirley, Birmingham. Special attention was paid to the necessity for obtaining plants of a natural dwarf habit and which were free branching and flowered abundantly.

The success of the work done in this connection can be measured by the fact that there are now more than a dozen named varieties of Lilliputs, varying in height from 6 to 8 inches. A further indication of success is found in the fact that, as stated by Woolmans, whereas the first varieties sent out produced about 150 flowers, subsequent varieties have been known to carry almost a thousand blooms on 8 inch high plants.

There is definitely a place for these dwarf varieties, for they are excellent for bedding and pot culture and have no difficulty to satisfy requirements.

Cultural routine is simple. Cuttings from short jointed shoots an inch or so long are rooted during February and March in the normal way. These can be boxed or put into small pots. Use an ordinary good compost, nothing very rich, for it is sturdy growth that is needed in the early and through all stages of development. Once growth begins, it will be found that the little plants will produce side shoots very freely so that no pinching out is needed. If the plants are to be kept in pots, they must be given the larger sizes as growth proceeds, until they reach the 6 inch size in which they will bloom. In pots, they are proving excellent market subjects, and local florists are often glad to purchase them. The usual watch must be kept for pests so that they can be dealt with before they gain a hold.

Plants can be put into the open ground about the second week in May, spacing them 2½ to 3 feet apart. There they will grow into healthy specimens for lifting in September, as soon as the buds begin to show colour. One great advantage the Lilliputs have as lifting subjects, is that the foliage being small there is rarely any wilting or flagging, which almost always occurs with the larger leaved types.

Among really good varieties, all of which produce dainty double flowers are: Bashful, bronze-red; Emu, rich rose; Happy, clear yellow; Honeybird, orange-amber; Isis, pink; Osiris, mauve; Pheasant, strawberry-red; Pimpernel, chestnut; Redbreast, red, and Tom Tit, yellow. The latter will often go on blooming well into November.

PERPETUAL FLOWERING

Another interesting section also raised by Messrs. H. Woolman Ltd., is the one known as the Perpetual Flowering chrysanthemum. Although the colour range is at present limited, it is certainly not beyond the powers of the raisers to bring out new varieties should the demand warrant it. The plants grow about a foot high, the individual flowers being around 4 inches in diameter. Cultivation does not require anything special; in fact, the plants can be grown in exactly the same way as the early flowering varieties.

These perpetuals are first class for bedding and do not need stopping, while, like the Lilliputs, they are admirable for pots. They have the further asset that the flowers can be used in various aspects of floral work.

This section is justly described as perpetual, since the cuttings can be rooted at any time during the year. Rooted in January, the plants will flower in March in small pots, and when this flowering period is over new basal shoots appear. These are potted up, and when they in turn flower, the whole process is repeated.

HARVEST GIANTS

A new type of garden chrysanthemum has been raised by the American firm of George J. Ball Inc. There are a number of varieties and these are known as Harvest Giants. They flower in September, and the raisers claim them to be the largest garden varieties in cultivation.

The plants should be grown in full sun, for partial shade delays flowering. They should be disbudded both to encourage earlier flowering and to obtain bigger blooms. These strong growing plants will develop up to 3 feet high and they are now available in this country. Among the sorts to be had are: Full Moon, pure white, up to 6 inches in diameter; Golden Arrow, rich golden-yellow; Indian Summer, striking deep bronze, up to $6\frac{1}{2}$ inches in diameter; Pink Haze, shell-pink; September Song, compact growing with rose-pink flowers, and White Frost, chalk-white, free flowering up to 6 inches in diameter with semi-curving blooms.

The Japanese have long been famed for their interest and skill in floral art. Because of this, growers in that country have been keen to raise and distribute new flowers. They have been successful in this, and as one would expect they have given considerable attention to the chrysanthemum. Among their fairly recent achievements, is the perfecting of three new and attractive strains of chrysanthemums which need the same culture as the greenhouse decorative varieties as outlined in Chapter 15.

BRUSH CHRYSANTHEMUMS

The varieties in the first section are known as the Brush chrysanthemums. This is because the flowers are shaped like an artist's brush, the thread like petals, up to 2 inches in length, being very much after the style of the bristles in a brush. It is recommended that the top growth should be pinched out in April and the plants then allowed to break naturally for second crowns.

The plants are available to name, taking in such colours as scarlet, pink, golden-yellow, lavender, rosy-pink and white.

NEW FANTASY

Another unusual type of chrysanthemum from Japan has become known as the New Fantasy selection. They have what may be described as a typically Japanese appearance, the petals being spidery, quilled and often spoon-shaped. They are particularly suitable for general floral art, and when used for house decoration, they never cease to give interest. These, too, are for greenhouse cultivation and may be treated in the same way as the November decorative varieties.

There are a number of named sorts including Bendigo, pink; Purple Cloud, purple; Raynham Gold, rich yellow, and Isobel Hodson, yellow. The latter, and several others, have long quilled petals, so shaped and placed that they are often known as Honeysuckle chrysanthemums.

MINIATURE ANEMONE FLOWERS

Then there is a group of miniature anemone-flowered sorts. These again are excellent for house decoration, their daintiness making them interesting and attractive on sight. The plants are grown in the ordinary way and allowed to break naturally for the second bud. There is really no need to disbud them at all, since their great beauty is enhanced by their sprays of bloom. Colours available include yellow, pink, scarlet, lavender and white.

SPOON VARIETIES

Another most unusual section is known as the Spoon chrysanthemum. These are for growing in the garden, or they may be grown in pots during the summer and taken indoors in the autumn. Of American origin, the colours of these very interesting novelties are really most beautiful.

RAYONNANTES

By no means new, the Rayonnante chrysanthemums have unusual, yet artistic, looking blooms. These are distinguished by their thread like, or rolled, quilled petals which are long and thin. Because of their lightness of form, they are much liked by those interested in all types of floral decorative art. Not only are the individual blooms sought after but the Rayonnantes are very decorative when grown as sprays.

One of the difficulties with these plants in the past was that so many of the flowers were weak in the 'neck'. Undoubtedly this is why they have not previously been grown as much as they deserve to be. Oddly enough, the Rayonnantes grown by the Dutch and which come into Covent Garden and other flower markets always seem to have stronger stems which take up water well, and therefore the flowers last longer.

Certainly British growers have always been able to produce bigger blooms, but the stems have been thin. Perhaps it is that the Dutch grow their plants outdoors for a longer period before bringing them under glass. This would seem to account for the brownish coloured, harder stems of their blooms which, however, are a greenish colour at the top. The flowers marketed by the British growers nearly always seem to be entirely green, which possibly is why they are weaker at the top or 'neck'.

However, there have been considerable improvements of late, and the plants now available are definitely worth growing. They require the same culture as the decoratives and they can be flowered with very little heat.

The colours generally available are, bronze, deep pink, yellow and white, while the green Rayonnante is one which ought to be grown where something unusual is required for indoor decoration.

Among the other spidery and thread petalled varieties which are sometimes available are the following named sorts, all well worth growing where something out of the ordinary is wanted: Bertie Bindon, white; Hiawatha, pink; King of Plumes, yellow; Mrs Carter, yellow, and Sam Caswell, pink. These are excellent for cutting and for use in all manner of floral decorations.

As we might expect, the Japanese have always been interested in the chrysanthemum, and there is no doubt that they possess many types which are not known or grown elsewhere. Reference to the catalogue of any of the bigger seed firms in Japan, will show how they are growing numerous types almost unknown here, some of which are mentioned later. They seem also to raise many more strains from seed than the British growers and they seem especially attracted to the large spider type petalled varieties, claiming that 'spider' flowers 5 inches or more in diameter can easily be raised from seed.

EDIBLE CHRYSANTHEMUMS

Some time ago mention was made in a gardening paper of edible chrysanthemums. Many thought that this was a hoax.

But there are edible plants. Of some, the petals are eaten as a salad and are said to be of good flavour, although, it seems, that it is only particular varieties and those having many petals that have been and, still are, depended upon for eating. They are reckoned by some dieticians to have some medicinal value.

Much more widely used in Japan is the edible leaved chrysanthemum known as Shungiko. This has small deeply indented leaves, which are a bright colour and are lightly aromatic, being delicious when eaten as 'greens'.

In a Japanese book on chrysanthemums, there is reference to many varieties which are unknown in this country, or so it would seem from the descriptions given. For instance there are varieties, or sections, described as globular; piled up; clutching; thistle; double broad; deep flowered and mobile petalled or mad chrysanthemums, a species in which the petals appear to have been blown about into every angle and direction. Whatever these various names may signify, it does seem as though there are some sections of chrysanthemums which we in Britain have not yet had an opportunity of growing.

SCENTED CHRYSANTHEMUMS

Lastly in this chapter of unusual or less common varieties, we must mention perfume. For long it has been said that if only we could have scent in the chrysanthemum, with all its other good points, not forgetting the very large colour range, and the long lasting qualities of the blooms, we could have a well nigh perfect flower.

It is, therefore, good to know that work is already being done by Messrs. Woolman, and some success has definitely been achieved in endeavours to breed perfume into the flowers. It will be a long time before scented chrysanthemums become available, but already one variety, Violet Queen, has been distributed on a limited scale. It is very pleasing to know that this is so. We can be sure that those who are working to produce a range of scented varieties are sparing no effort in order to make a further advance in the progress of the chrysanthemum, and to give added pleasure in growing these good tempered plants to a very large number of people.

Chrysanthemum frutescens var., Jamaica Primrose, was found growing in a garden near the Blue Mountains of Jamaica. It is believed, by some, to be a sport or a reversion of the parent stock of the once widely grown Marguerite, which was known as the Paris Daisy.

The Jamaica Primrose makes an excellent bedding subject and can be planted out of doors in May. It continues to flower until November, and is also valuable when cut, lasting well in water.

The usual growing routine is to lift the stools in the late autumn and treat them like the normal early chrysanthemum. The stock plants and the cuttings can also be grown without heat where the plants are not required early.

Nothing special in the way of culture is needed, for this plant grows well in ordinary good soil and does not need staking or stopping. Although it is always best to leave just a few flowers when cutting, it is noticeable that if the growths are cut back completely, a fresh supply of shoots will come on very quickly and soon produce flowers, although, of course, not after the middle of September.

This plant has received an Award of Merit from the Royal Horticultural Society after a trial at Wisley, which is an indication that it is a plant worth growing.

CHAPTER TWENTY-FIVE

Chrysanthemum Maximum

OFTEN KNOWN as the Ox-Eye Daisy, *Chrysanthemum leucanthemum* is a native plant which has played an important part in developing many of the popular garden varieties of the Shasta daisies, now so much grown for market work.

While most of these are now classed as *C. maximum*, a Pyrean plant which has long been grown in this country, it is a fact that many of the modern varieties are derived from *C. leucanthemum*. For instance, Esther Read, perhaps the most popular variety of all *C. maximum*, came directly from *C. leucanthemum*, in this way. In 1933, the late Mr. H. P. Read noticed that in the yellow centre of a flower of the latter species there appeared a number of small crippled petals. He at once realised the possibilities of such a happening and commenced work on breeding a really good double Shasta daisy. When after eleven years and the growing of hundreds of thousands of seedlings, plus a great many disappointments, success came, the stalk was too weak to hold up the flower properly.

A further three or four years elapsed before the really strong stalk, as we know it today, was obtained. So high was the standard aimed at by H. P. Read that he sent only three varieties to the R.H.S. and these three Esther Read, Horace Read and Pauline Read, all received an Award of Merit. The first two sorts remain as the most popular *C. maximums* grown today, but Pauline Read, a deep creamy-yellow, was never offered to the public because of its habit of flowering itself to death, thus weakening its constitution.

Esther Read, as now distributed, has stiff upright stems 18 inches high and large, fully double white flowers, having a pale lemon centre. It bunches, packs and travels well and is altogether an excellent cut flower from June to September, sometimes later, while as a border plant it is invaluable.

Since this is by far the most widely grown variety, the following detailed information is given to enable best results to be obtained.

Culture. This variety likes and really thrives on a very rich, well drained soil. It can be grown very successfully in heavy Essex clay, in light sandy loam, and anything between, so long as nourishment and good drainage are there. Although really quite hardy, Esther Read dislikes cold, wet winters. This is the reason the plant sometimes dies off. It seems natural that since the plant is so vigorous and produces a wealth of bloom over a very long period that by the autumn the vigour of the stools is sapped. When there is excessive wet and cold, the weakened plants easily become subject to the rotting of the older tissues. Where the stools have become almost exhausted, the whole plant will sometimes die right away.

As with all types of plants, it is essential to obtain the true stock. Unfortunately, now that a number of years have elapsed since Esther Read was raised, there are many stocks being offered which are not the true variety at all. In many cases, they are really sports and often considerably less hardy than the variety whose name they bear. This accounts for the fact that it is sometimes wrongly alleged that Esther Read is not winter hardy.

Esther can be distinguished by its natural characteristics. It has thin, wiry stems, which vary from 12 to 18 inches in length and which are covered with minute, yet visible hairs. All the sports as far as is known, have much stiffer, unyielding stems, which in each case are shiny with no visible hairy growths. The flowers of these variations, however, are very similar to the true type, hence the frequent error in distributing the wrong stocks, especially when the purchasers of planting sets are not familiar with the true Esther Read.

Feeding. It seems an impossibility to overfeed this sort, and in the preparation of the planting site very generous quantities of manure or other organic materials should be well worked in.

Diseases. This variety is not known to suffer from any disease. Care should be taken to plant up a clean, young stock. Then, as previously indicated, the only likelihood of trouble is as a result of cold and wet, when sometimes, due to bacterial action on weak, exhausted stools, black-rot sets in. This, however, cannot really be classed as a disease, since it is only nature's way of dealing with exhausted plants.

Hardiness. It is again emphasised that Esther Read is perfectly hardy when grown under normal healthy conditions in well drained ground. In damp, cold districts it is better to protect with cloches or similar glass covering. Even so, plants have been known to withstand zero temperatures on heavy land without any loss.

Propagation. The safest way to propagate is by removing rooted shoots during late summer, and getting these established in clean, weed free land, where, once established, they will winter perfectly well. The plants to be propagated are best dis-bloomed about July to encourage new growth. Well water the stools until the necessary cuttings are taken.

Flowering Time. One of the important virtues of Esther Read, which has long been recognised by growers, is its ability to produce an abundance of really good blooms over a period of several months. Flowers can be had from a healthy plantation from June until October, and there are few subjects which are so floriferous. It is still the earliest flowering variety in commerce.

Planting Distance. According to the space and soil available, the young plants may be set at anything from 12 to 18 inches apart. Where substantial quantities are being grown, a wider distance should be allowed after every three rows to facilitate the easy cleaning of the beds and the gathering of the blooms. To provide a really early crop of flowers, Esther Read may be grown very successfully under glass.

Horace Read, growing 2 feet or more, is another really outstanding variety, having very stout upright stems and producing in abundance, plenty of pure white fully double flowers which from the true stock, often reach 6 to 7 inches in diameter, making a first class border and florists' flower. As a result of lack of supervision, some stocks at present being distributed have degenerated and do not give really good blooms, but the stock available from the raisers' firm is still from the original plants and absolutely true.

One of the most amazing *C. maximum* introductions since Esther Read, is the variety Jenifer Read, a sport from Esther, which was shown for the first time in July 1950. As a commercial variety it is invaluable, since it extends the cutting period until September. It is very hardy and succeeds where it has been found impossible to winter Esther. The outer petals are much broader than the latter variety but of the same intense white, the lemon centre of Esther being replaced by a deep marigold middle, making a very striking flower.

The bushy plants grow to a height of 3 feet, the actual stiff cutting stems averaging 18 to 24 inches throughout the season, no side budding being necessary. Jenifer Read has the unusual habit of making a wealth of short growth in September, the leaves so formed, apparently providing protection and enabling the plants to survive the winter without harm. This variety has been patented in America and is also popular in Australia and other countries.

Wirral Pride is another good sort, the clean white flowers being carried on stout 3 foot stems, the full anemone-like centre making it most attractive. Wirral Supreme is also a very fine variety, the bushy plants growing up to $3\frac{1}{2}$ feet high and producing fully double, pure white blooms of great value for cutting and border display. Some of the older Shasta daisies, while not reaching the standard of the varieties already mentioned, are certainly good garden plants. These include the continental variety, Beauté Nivelloise, a hardy sort with overlapping, pure white fimbriated petals and a small yellow disc; Gruppenstolz, large snow-white blooms of good substances; Mayfield Giant, large pure white flowers on 4 foot stems, and Phyllis Smith, a beautiful sort resembling a Japanese chrysanthemum with snow-white narrow petals, twisted and twirled in a most fantastic manner. Other good varieties available include the following:

THOMAS KILLEN. Award of Merit in the R.H.S. Trials. Large pure white anemone-centred flower $5\frac{1}{2}$ inches across. Strong grower with stout stems carrying the large flowers easily. Should make a first class market flower.

JOHN MURRAY. Flowers fully double, pure white and free from defect – could easily be mistaken for double white early flowering chrysanthemum. Flowers produced on long stems, averaging $4\frac{1}{2}$ to 5 inches across, they last well on or off the plant, even in hot weather. Flowers from July to frost.

MARGARET MURRAY. As new improved Wirral Supreme, having a large flower. Commences flowering earlier and cropping for a longer period.

MARION BISLAND. Fine new single. Refined flower on long stiff stems, will keep well in water. Needs no staking, standing all weathers. Suitable as a market cut flower. Travels well.

SNOWBALL. Dwarf double variety. Strong stiff stems – flowers appear as a neat round ball. Good for border or cut flower, first rate for market.

MOONLIGHT. A new and important variety for the market grower and for house decoration. The best description is a Wirral Supreme with a yellow flush, making a very attractive flower. Moonlight is a very descriptive name, as this is the nearest one can get to its appearance at a distance. The flower is larger than Wirral Supreme and has the same perfect formation and long stiff stem. Large quantities of flowers have been sent to the wholesale markets where they sell readily, and the demand appears to be increasing. This variety will make a wonderful companion to Cobham Gold, as it is much earlier.

GUSSIE. A novel double shaggy type with short frills, now becoming so popular with the ladies. Strong stem with delightful flowers of pure white.

MELISSA. Another delightful shaggy type with pure white flowers, but with long frills.

SCRUFFY. Pure white shaggy flowers of lovely untidiness.

GOLIATH. Huge large flowered single, outstanding and worth growing.

MOUNT EVEREST. Large single white of fine form, lasting well when cut.

IAN MURRAY. Strong growing anemone-centred single, good for garden or cutting.

SNOW PRINCESS. A new double-fringed variety with very attractive flowers, unlike any other variety at present available.

AGLAIA. Fully double, pure white shaggy flowers, so popular for house decoration.

DROITWICH BEAUTY. Another large shaggy type of flower with fine white petals. A market variety having long stiff stems.

There are others in cultivation but those detailed are the very best available.

A fairly recently introduced *Chrysanthemum maximum*, is Cobham Gold, which is, in fact, the first really coloured variety ever offered. Of outstanding merit, it has much the same habit as Esther Read, but with its liquid gold colouring it has certainly made an appeal to all flower lovers. It is an excellent commercial plant, providing an abundance of flowers over a long period, while, because its blooms are carried on upright stiff stems, it suffers very little damage from rain splash, neither is it easily damaged by winds.

Cobham Gold which was raised by Lord Darnley, was first distributed by Mr. F. G. Read. When exhibited at the

R.H.S. Hall, it was well received, but did not get an award since it is of a similar shade to Pauline Read which did receive the award, although it has never been marketed. At the bunching stage, Cobham Gold looks a rich butter colour, deepening towards the centre.

Joan Reeves is a still newer variety having yellow flushed flowers, and this, too, seems likely to become popular with both gardeners and florists.

All *C. maximums* like a soil in which there is stable manure and potash, and none present any cultural difficulties.

CHAPTER TWENTY-SIX

Annual Chrysanthemums

A<small>LTHOUGH</small> unable to compete in size, colour range or lasting qualities with their much better known perennial relatives, the annual chrysanthemums are nevertheless worthy of consideration for either cut flower or border edging purposes.

The annuals are extremely easy to grow, and produce over a long period an abundance of showy blooms, so valuable for garden and house decoration. It is true to say that without both the flowers and ornamental foliage of the annual chrysanthemums, the summer border would often be of less interest.

In addition, these annuals are valuable for growing under glass, and by sowing early, a brilliant display of colour can be procured in the greenhouse from the middle of April onwards.

For successful indoor cultivation, cool treatment is essential. Fussing the young plants or applying too much heat will result in weak growing, thin specimens which will never really recover from the initial wrong treatment, or flower so readily as plants grown on sturdily. There are numerous species, but we will mention only those of which seed is obtainable.

The three main species of annual chrysanthemums are *C. carinatum*, *C. coronarium* and *C. segetum*. The first named is frequently referred to as tricolor, of which there are today many handsome forms. The species itself has white petals which are bright yellow at the base, the dark purple centre making up the three colours, hence the term tricolor. Among the best named varieties of *C. tricolor*, growing about 18 inches high, are *Burridgeanum* with yellowish foliage, while *carinatum* Northern Star, has large white petals with a yellow ring at the base and a blackish-maroon central disc, and The Sultan has bronzy-red shades of yellow with a brown disc.

It is, however, the mixtures of *C. carinatum* or *tricolor*, which are particularly effective, either when growing alone or placed among other annuals. Apart from a wide range of three coloured single flowers, there are semi-double, double and beautifully fringed strains.

All the *Chrysanthemum coronarium* varieties have finely cut foliage, and while the species itself has pale yellow, semi-double flowers, there are numerous garden varieties which have been derived from it and which are attractive in every way. These include Golden Glory, growing 2 feet high with large single, rich yellow flowers, excellent for cutting; Golden Crown, often 3 feet or more high, the double yellow flowers having prettily quilled petals; Golden Queen and Primrose Queen both form compact bushes not more than 18 inches high, and Tom Thumb Golden Gem is 12 to 15 inches high, making a useful pot plant.

Chrysanthemum segetum, which has two forms, *grandiflorum* with larger flowers, and *pumilum* of more compact habit, is really quite common and often found in cornfields, being sometimes referred to as the 'corn marigold'. This species has small single yellow flowers, but has, as the result of much patient selection, given rise to many beautiful forms, all growing about 18 inches high. Among these are Eldorado, large single, bright yellow with black centre; Evening Star, golden-yellow with dark disc; Morning Star, soft primrose with golden centre and decorative glaucous-green foliage. This variety has received an R.H.S. Award of Merit.

All of these cut flower varieties respond well to autumn sowing, and although as with other subjects, there may be some winter losses, the majority of plants come through well. They make extra bushy plants which flower earlier and longer than spring sown specimens. In addition, the colour tones appear to be much more pronounced. These flowers bunch well and are useful for market work. It is advisable to strip off the lower leaves before standing the stems in water. This will prevent any messiness when the stems are taken out and also prevent the water from becoming fouled.

Much less common is *C. fontanesii* of Mediterranean origin, with slender, branched cut-edged leaves. Growing about 12 inches high, it produces many small white flowers and is an excellent edging plant.

C. multicaule is from Algeria, although it has been grown in Britain for about seventy-five years. This, too, has deeply toothed leaves, its 6 to 10 inch stems bearing bright yellow flowers. Useful for edging purposes, it also does well in pots in the cold greenhouse, where a short growing plant is wanted.

C. nivelli, from Morocco, makes a bushy plant with deeply cut leaves. The small white flowers up to an inch in diameter, are carried on 10 to 12 inch stems, and are interesting because of the soft woolly hairs on the undersides of the petals.

C. parthenium is the British Feverfew, growing 12 to 18 inches in height and having small white flowers and well cut, hairy leaves. It is often known and catalogued as *Matricaria eximia*, but it is not really worth growing as a garden plant. Strictly speaking, this is a perennial plant, but it is usually treated as an annual, since it flowers well the first year from seed. It is, however, the double forms, normally listed as *var. flore pleno*, that are so attractive as edging plants. The three best known varieties are Silver Ball, Lemon Ball and Golden Ball. Then there are two forms of *C. parthenium* which are grown for their attractive foliage. They are *var. aureum*, with yellow foliage, and *var. crispum*, of which the leaves are attractively crimped and curled.

C. viscidi-hirtum also known as *C. viscosum*, is a native of North Africa and of Spain. It is best suited for growing in the wild garden for the yellow flowers are rather coarse, the well cut foliage being covered with sticky hairs making it unpleasant to touch.

All the annual chrysanthemums should be grown in irregular groups. They are very free and long flowering and of most easy culture. They are very adaptable as far as soil is concerned, although they prefer a light, well drained, sunny situation. Even when these conditions are not provided, once established, the plants produce their blooms most abundantly.

Although they may appear to be but poor relations of the border growing perennial chrysanthemums, the annuals should not be neglected. Whether one is concentrating on a formal effect or on something of a more natural appearance, these annuals are worthy of a place.

CHAPTER TWENTY-SEVEN

Diseases of the Chrysanthemum

GROWN UNDER good hygienic conditions, the chrysanthemum is not likely to be much troubled by diseases. A number of possibilities are mentioned, so that they may be recognised and dealt with before they gain a hold.

POWDERY MILDEW

This is probably the most common trouble likely to be encountered. It is in evidence in some seasons much more than in others, especially on pot plants in the greenhouse or conservatory. It is easily recognised by the white mealy, powdery growth on the leaves, particularly on the undersides. This is not only unsightly but affected plants lose vigour and the leaves turn brown and fall off. Some varieties are more susceptible than others. It is a mistake to think that mildew can only appear under moist circumstances, in fact, it is often encouraged by dry root conditions. If the soil is kept normally moist and a good air circulation is maintained around the plants, there should be little real trouble from this disease.

Fortunately, powdery mildew is easily controlled provided the proper measures are taken early enough, but if left unchecked, it will affect all the foliage as well as the blooms, while it can completely ruin a batch of cuttings.

There is reason to believe that overfed plants, brought up on artificial fertilisers are more susceptible to the spores of this fungus disease than plants grown under a more natural feeding programme. A watch should be kept on the plants while they are outdoors; in fact, it is a good plan to give a preventive spray or dusting of green sulphur or copper from time to time. This should certainly be done immediately prior to housing.

White oil emulsion used alone or with colloidal copper will not only destroy mildew, but give a dark green healthy appearance to the leaves.

Karathane, a fungicide of American origin, has also given first class results in controlling powdery mildew on a wide range of plants. A preparation known as Fungex is used by some of the bigger growers. This is applied at the rate of 1 fluid ounce dissolved in 3 gallons of water and has proved very satisfactory in clearing even bad attacks.

In the greenhouse, a sulphur vaporiser is most valuable. This is a small drum which holds a container having a funnel shaped top. Flowers of sulphur are placed in the container which is warmed by a lamp, leading to the vaporising of the sulphur which effectively clears mildew.

BLOTCH OR LEAF SPOT

This disease, of which the proper name is *Septoria chrysanthemella*, seems more likely to occur on plants which have made 'soft' growth due to the use of too much nitrogeneous fertiliser. It is recognised by the brown or blackish spots or blotches on the leaves, which, when the attack is bad, may fall off. Although it seems to be more prevalent on outdoor plants, the disease does occur in the greenhouse, especially when ventilation is poor. The fungus spores are spread by splashed water and this is why the disease is less severe in dry weather, although the spores can be carried on cuttings and divisions. It seems to work from the base of the stems upwards, which perhaps is why it is sometimes mistaken for eelworm.

All affected leaves should be removed and burnt and the plants sprayed with Bordeaux Mixture paying special attention to the lower parts of the plants.

RUST

This appears in the form of red, rusty looking pustules on the lower surfaces of the leaves. Fairly common, it can be a really serious disease in wet seasons. At these times, the plants are of a very poor appearance. As the fungus develops within the leaf tissues, the surface is eventually ruptured, setting free the disease spores enabling them to settle on other healthy foliage and repeat the whole process. They are easily transported by wind and water splashings. The disease can be carried over from one season to another on the leaves of young growths that develop after the plants have finished growing and where the new shoots are used for cuttings.

Since the spores can only live on the leaves, this is a good reason for cutting all old stems down to ground level and for burning all leaves and green growths. Wettable sulphur sprays in one of their many forms give good control providing one makes sure to contact all parts of the plant. Some growers believe that rust is more likely to occur as a result of some severe check, possibly root starvation or even continual wet soil conditions.

Propagation should never be carried out from plants suspected of having had rust disease. Some varieties seem more susceptible than others, and unfortunately these include such good sorts as the Favourites, Loveliness and Friendly Rival.

CROWN OR LEAFY GALL

This is caused by a microscopic bacterium, *Corynebacterium fascians* and affected plants produce short, thick, twisted, distorted buds and shoots at the base of the stems. Since there is no known cure, the infected plants should be burned and not left in the soil or lying about. The bacterium is very infectious, so that after contacting diseased plants, boxes, tools, including knives, as well as the hands, should be sterilised before they touch healthy plants.

New stocks of chrysanthemums should not be grown for at least a couple of years in ground which has carried a diseased crop.

FLOWER SCORCH

This shows itself as small brown markings or spots on the outer florets. These marks increase in size until the whole flower withers. It is most likely to occur under glass where there is a high humidity. Control is by making the atmosphere drier and by using a good fungicide.

WILT

This is now a fairly common disease, caused by the fungus *Verticillium dahliae*. It is first seen by the lower leaves becoming pale and limp, and in bad attacks, the whole plant wilts, the leaves becoming brown and lifeless. Infection appears to occur at the roots, and the fungus may be carried in cuttings so slightly affected that it is not noticed at propagating time.

This is yet another reason why the greatest of care should be taken in securing cuttings from really healthy stools. Affected plants do not recover and should be destroyed. Certainly they should never be divided and re-planted. When an attack of Wilt has been confirmed, do not grow chrysanthemums in the same soil for two or three years at least, and always buy fresh stock from a reliable, known source.

BOTRYTIS

There are many types of botrytis, and all parts of a plant may be affected by one or more of these fungus troubles. Grey Mould or the Damping of chrysanthemum blooms can cause serious losses of both indoor and outdoor grown plants. This particular fungus is identified as *Botrytis cinerea*, which will attack many different cultivated plants. In the open ground, wet conditions enable this disease to develop rapidly so that some protection from rain is desirable. It also occurs under glass where damp conditions favour its development. This is one reason why it is unwise to attempt to save the fuel bill by failing to provide some heat from November onwards. Here again, it is thought that the frequent use of nitrogenous fertilisers renders the plants more susceptible to attack. Although the lining of greenhouses with polythene to maintain humid conditions during propagating time is quite effective, such a lining must be removed when late flowering chrysanthemums are being grown in the glasshouse. If left, damping is encouraged.

Since it is not possible to prevent the entry of the air-borne spores into the greenhouse, the aim must be to create conditions where they cannot thrive. This means the provision of such an amount of heat as will reduce humidity and will ensure a buoyant atmosphere. Good ventilation is also needed to maintain regular air movement.

It has been found that botrytis spores cannot develop when the night temperature drops to 40 degrees F., however wet and misty the atmosphere may be. This is why late flowering outdoor chrysanthemums do not become attacked by botrytis and will sometimes go on blooming really well until quite late in the year.

Unfortunately, it is a temperature of 70 to 75 degrees F, which allows the spores to flourish, and this is the amount of warmth frequently available during the early winter months. The answer, therefore, is in avoiding a close damp atmosphere by proper ventilation. Some protection can be given by covering the blooms with greaseproof bags, details of which are given in the chapter on bagging or covering the flowers. Affected blooms must always be removed on sight in order to prevent the spread of the fungus spores to other flowers. There are several 'dusts' including Orthocide which are said to prevent the spores from working, if they are applied when the blooms begin to show colour.

VIRUS DISEASES

During the last twenty years or so, we have become very virus conscious. Quite a number of diseases affecting human beings and animals are known to arise from virus infection. Viruses are, unfortunately, prevalent in the plant world too, and a number of our most popular flowers such as the dahlia and sweet pea are sometimes attacked and ruined.

There must be few growers of chrysanthemums who have not heard of or experienced in their plants, mosaic mottle or spotted wilt. There are in fact a dozen or more different forms of virus liable to attack chrysanthemums, but some of them are very rare. Others, of course, are both widespread and very harmful.

It seems evident that some varieties are more susceptible than others; the 'Sweetheart' family, for instance, has shown signs of being easy prey to different viruses. Other sorts seem resistant in varying degrees. This does not mean that the varieties showing some degree of resistance are not likely to succumb to these troubles. In fact, it could be that such sorts are really masking the symptoms, and in so doing may actually act as a source of infection to others.

Although a considerable amount of research has been done, there is still much to learn regarding the various virus diseases. It is important to find out similarities or relationships to viruses known in other crops and more about the ways in which they spread.

The most common and the most serious form is that known as the tomato aspermy virus. Unfortunately, it does not show its presence in the foliage, so it cannot be seen at the cutting stage. The flowers of affected varieties are greatly damaged, they are smaller than usual, the petals being twisted and otherwise misshapen, many of the florets becoming spiky. Another pointer to the disease is that the blooms of the red, bronze and pink varieties are streaked or marked with a lighter colour. It is, therefore, most important to regularly look over the flowers and to rogue out any plants which are at all suspicious looking.

Aspermy virus is spread by aphids, and it can also infect other families of plants.

STUNT VIRUS

As the name implies, this causes stunting or dwarfing of the plants, and in really severe cases plants may only reach half their normal height. Affected specimens flower early, but the blooms are small and of poor quality. This disease is reckoned by some growers to have been largely introduced into this country by the coming of some of the American varieties. It is infectious and can be spread by the cutting knife and during disbudding, although so far, no insect has been reported as being the carrier of the disease.

Affected plants should be removed so that the foliage of adjacent plants is not contacted, and the hands should be washed immediately after touching such plants.

SPOTTED WILT

This is a virus which is known to attack many cultivated and wild plants. It appears to have varying symptoms. With some varieties of chrysanthemums, the lower foliage may die off and there is a yellowing in the veins on the leaves. In others, there are various lighter lines in the foliage and these eventually spread to irregular blotches.

Tomatoes and some ornamental greenhouse plants seem to carry the infection, which is often spread from plant to plant by thrips.

VIRUS B

Often known as Mild Mosaic, this is also a very widespread disease. It shows itself by faint leaf mottlings or by the main veins looking pale at the early cutting stage, but these are less prominent as the plant grows. Sometimes there are no obvious signs that the plants are infected.

CUCUMBER MOSAIC

This, in many ways, is similar to aspermy virus. It is most easily seen in the flowers, the buds opening slowly, and when the ray florets do show they are frequently distorted, rolled inwards or they are twisted and often streaked with yellow. Sometimes the flowers fail to open at all. The vigour of the plants does not seem to be affected very much, and even when the flowers are greatly attacked, there is no obvious trace of the disease in the leaves. Both early and late varieties may be infected, including those popular varieties, American Beauty, Baldock's Crimson and Friendly Rival.

Cucumber mosaic is transmitted by aphids, and many growers dip their cuttings in a nicotine or similar solution before inserting them. Infected plants should be destroyed, and when buying cuttings or plants every precaution should be taken to ensure really healthy stock.

Unfortunately, late season infections often show few or no symptoms, which is another reason for propagating only from healthy stock which has been examined at flowering time.

It is not sufficient just to discard unhealthy looking plants.

Fairly recently, a great step forward has been made in regard to keeping down or eradicating virus diseases. This is known as Heat Therapy. The story begins about ten years ago when virus in chrysanthemum stocks had risen to an almost alarming degree. This is thought to have been largely due to the introduction of so many American varieties, especially the spray sorts, which, it was discovered, were often anything but clean. We are not, of course, suggesting that this is the source of all virus troubles – it is certainly not so.

After various experiments and tests had been made, chiefly at the Plant Pathology Laboratory at Harpenden, it was found that certain viruses could be eradicated by growing them in what was at first called a 'Hot-Box', for at least three but preferably four weeks, in a temperature of 97 degrees F. After this time, tiny tip cuttings were taken and grown on under clean, insect-free conditions. This method, however, did not really allow a sufficient number of cuttings to be obtained for commercial purposes.

It was then that the well known chrysanthemum specialist, Mr. Frank Rowe, of Wellington, Somerset, took an active interest in the matter, and on a commercial scale. He provided a suitable propagating house of about 100 feet by 15 feet, and this was made into the necessary heat chamber.

Since for the experiment it was necessary to maintain the correct temperature of 97 degrees F., even during the coldest weather, the house was lined with polythene film. Extra heating pipes were put in and the oil fired boiler was operated by a rod thermostat set at the required 97 degrees F. A special blower was installed to condition the air and prevent 'cold spots' among the plants due to transpiration. Muslin was placed over the ventilators to make them insect proof.

The house was filled with plants several inches tall, and after they had been subjected to the necessary high temperature of 97 degrees F. for nearly a month, tip cuttings ¼ inch long were taken. Even when these tips were white or pale yellow, because of the forcing conditions, they soon became a natural green colour after insertion.

After these tip cuttings have rooted they must be kept under insect-proof conditions for a time, for greenfly is able to transmit aspermy virus which is one of the worst forms.

Although Heat Therapy stocks have been available for so few years, they are now depended upon by many growers, some of whom now offer special Heat Therapy raised stock to the general public.

Reports seem to indicate that far from the treatment weakening the stocks, the plants are healthy, vigorous and represent a great step forward. Some growers have reported that treated plants have produced better flowers and an improved leaf colour. Certain varieties which previously had the habit of losing their leaves no longer do this, and there has, generally speaking, been an all round improvement in growth. A few varieties which have produced rolled, instead of flat petals, have had this failing corrected through heat therapy, which is obviously something which has done and is doing, great things for the chrysanthemum.

CHAPTER TWENTY-EIGHT

Pests of the Chrysanthemum

IT WOULD indeed be wonderful if we could record that a plant so accommodating as the chrysanthemum was free from attacks by pests. While this plant, when given ordinary good growing conditions, is not specially liable to be attacked, the fact is that there are upwards of fifty different pests that have been known to cause trouble.

From this one might possibly wonder whether it is really worth trying to grow chrysanthemums at all with so many enemies to contend with, but of course, the average grower sees only a very, very small number of pests in the course of the year.

While we shall not refer to all the pests which may at one time or another attack chrysanthemums, we are mentioning quite a lot. Although this does not mean that they are bound to be troublesome, they are referred to so that the grower may know of their existence in order that he can recognise them easily and be able to deal with them effectively before they gain a hold.

As the result of scientific work during recent years, the control of pests is easier than it was a few decades ago, but undoubtedly the best approach to the matter is a cultural routine which aims at prevention rather than one which goes all out to cure, however effective such measures may be.

There are a few pests which are almost certain to appear, and these are often 'common' ones which are present on many plants and which, therefore, can easily travel to chrysanthemum plants in the same garden, field or greenhouse.

It is general knowledge that well grown plants kept under healthy conditions are less likely to be seriously affected than those which are in poor condition. Much can also be done by keeping down weeds many of which act as hosts to various pests providing, as it were, a stepping stone for the onslaughts.

Greenfly is one of the most persistent of pests, and because this is so there is much to be said for the regular preventive spraying of the plants. There are, of course, very many insecticides that one can use. Some growers stick to the chemical types such as D.D.T., H.E.T.P., Malathion and Gammexane, which, of course, are good in their own way. Gammexane is sold in several forms and under a number of proprietary names, including B.H.C., Lindex and Sybol. There is no doubt, however, that insecticides of vegetable origin, such as are relied upon by organic gardeners are particularly effective and safe. These include derris, quassia extract, pyrethrum and quassia. It is, of course, often the practice to mix gammexane with D.D.T., while some users believe that H.E.T.P. is stronger than nicotine, which also means that it must be used with extra care.

There are several forms of nicotine, all of which are poisonous and so need to be handled by responsible persons.

Aphids head the list of the more common pests which are likely to be seen year after year. Of these, greenfly, as we have already mentioned, is almost a certainty at some time or other, since there are few cultivated plants on which they do not settle. Apart from the actual damage they do, these aphids often act as carriers of virus diseases which have become much more prevalent in recent years and which have caused and are causing, a great deal of concern to chrysanthemum raisers.

So often these pests are on the plants before they are noticed and this is why it is advisable to give the plants sprayings of an insecticide even when they appear to be clean. Greenfly and other aphids settle on the undersides of the leaves, also on and in the growing tips of both young and established plants. At these points they suck the sap, harming growth and causing distortion. It is not only the disfiguration they cause that makes it important to get rid of them but the possibility of sap borne diseases being carried from plant to plant.

When and while the plants are outdoors, the sprays already mentioned may be applied. Aphids increase very rapidly so that it is necessary to spray regularly, particularly if the pests have been seen on the plants. It is really important to get rid of them before the flowers unfold for if greenflies get among the petals it is impossible to get rid of them all without causing damage to the blooms. There is reason to believe that greenfly and other aphids can build up an immunity against a particular insecticide if it is used for a long period. This is why it is a good plan to change the spray from time to time. Take care never to destroy ladybirds – the natural enemy of greenflies.

Rather more care is needed with the choice and application of insecticides in the greenhouse. Very often it is advisable if not essential, to take steps against the pests at the time the cuttings are taken. Some growers as a matter of routine, dip the cuttings in an insecticide before they are inserted in the compost. As the later sprayings are given, the entire plant must be wetted which includes the undersides of the leaves.

During recent years a number of smokes and aerosols have been introduced and fumigation by nicotine, properly done, is most effective. Some of these 'smokes' also destroy the persistent white fly.

Extreme care is needed if and when many of the modern insecticides are used. They are often strongly recommended, and there is no doubt that some of them at least, are most effective. These insecticides include malathion, parathion (which kills eelworm) and demeton-methyl. The latter will remain toxic for a considerable period.

CATERPILLARS

If present, even in small numbers, the caterpillars of various species of moths can cause considerable damage both to the leaves and blooms. In bad cases, the leaves may be stripped and the flower buds spoiled. Although caterpillars are liable to be present throughout the summer, they seem to appear most frequently on the late varieties after the plants have been moved from the open ground to the greenhouse. They are usually a greenish or grey-brown colour.

When seen, they can be hand picked, while D.D.T. is used by many growers, and this has proved to be thoroughly effective in keeping caterpillars from doing any great amount of harm. A good alternative which I prefer, is liquid derris or pyrethrum powder.

CAPSID BUGS

There are several species of these quick moving pests which do a tremendous amount of damage chiefly by sucking the sap from the plants. This leads to blindness, distortion of stems and shoots, mottled foliage and badly shaped flowers. Sometimes they attack the flower buds, resulting in a one sided bloom.

There appears to be two or more distinct species of Capsid Bug, and among their common names they are known as the Green Capsid Bug, the Potato Capsid, the Tarnished Plant Bug and the Bishop Bug.

In size, these bugs are about the same as the ordinary house fly, and although the life cycle of the different species varies, the harm they do and the measures we can take to keep them away, are identical.

One of the difficulties in getting rid of them is that they are able to settle and remain on various types of weeds and also fruit bushes. This is one good reason why the surrounds of the plot where chrysanthemums are growing should be kept free from weeds. They appear most freely from July to September and will, of course, also settle on other plants such as dahlias, so that even after one has taken precautions to keep the plants clean, repetition is necessary.

Spraying the plants and particularly the unopened buds with wettable D.D.T. seems to be the best remedy at present. Since often some of the bugs fall or are knocked off the plants, it is a good plan to sprinkle D.D.T. powder on the lower parts of the plants and also on the ground itself. During the summer, too, an occasional spraying of a good insecticide such as Derris or Sybol, should be given to the surrounding hedges or plants.

In the greenhouse, a low pressure aerosol of a pyrethrum base is effective, as are the more potent malathion sprays. The idea with these is to produce atmospheric destruction to the pests and not to direct the sprays straight on to the plants which might become marked.

BLOSSOM MIDGE

The yellow grubs of this pest feed on the flower buds which are prevented from opening. All attacked buds should be destroyed and the plants sprayed with derris or malathion; in fact, if this spraying is done as a routine measure, the pest is most unlikely to appear at all.

WHITE FLY

This is usually troublesome on plants in the greenhouse, although it is not unknown for them to attack plants growing outdoors too. They feed from the undersides of the leaves, weakening the plants. The sticky 'honey dew' they excrete encourages a black mould which further weakens the plants, besides making them look so unsightly.

There are a number of proprietary white fly destroyers. They must, however, be used with care and strictly in accordance with the manufacturer's instructions. Some preparations which are used for killing white fly on crops such as cucumbers and tomatoes would spoil the plants if used on chrysanthemums.

RED SPIDER MITE

This is another pest which thrives on the undersides of the leaves by sucking the sap, causing poor, weak growth. It is most likely to occur and persist, in hot dry temperatures so that much can be done in preventing such conditions. Among the various controls available, the azobenzine smokes have proved effective.

THE FROG HOPPER

This is a small brown insect which is fairly well known because of its ability to jump vigorously when disturbed. In its young stages, it is usually referred to as 'Cuckoo Spit' because of the froth with which it surrounds itself. It is of course a common pest which appears on many types of plants and here again it will often be found on near-by weeds from where it will migrate to chrysanthemums.

Both nicotine and D.D.T. sprays will destroy 'Cuckoo Spit' on contact. Several applications are usually necessary in order to deal with the pest in its various stages.

THRIPS

These tiny insects can do quite a lot of damage to chrysanthemum flowers which they will cause to shrivel if left to pursue their course. It is often possible to shake them out of the flowers, and if they are caused to fall on paper or cloth, this can be gathered up and burned.

Lindex, Sybol and D.D.T. have all proved effective in destroying these pests which seem more likely to appear during or after a hot, dry spell. For this reason, it is a good plan to give the plants a few sprayings of insecticide as a precaution rather than waiting for the pests to appear.

CHRYSANTHEMUM LEAF MINER

Almost everyone who has grown chrysanthemums must be familiar with the curling white or pale yellow lines on the upper surfaces of the leaves. This is caused by the maggots of a small brown fly known specifically as *Phytomza atricornis*. The female fly is able to puncture the surface of the leaves and then lays her eggs between the upper and lower leaf 'skins'. After the eggs hatch, the resultant maggots eat their way along the interior of the leaves, showing the white lines as they progress. The maggots can be clearly seen from the undersides of the affected foliage and should always be crushed. If left, they change into a pupa from which a fly emerges and the whole life cycle is repeated. If only a few leaves are affected, they can be taken off and burned. This is not possible where a good number of plants are attacked.

The aim must be to destroy the fly and so prevent eggs being laid. Various forms of nicotine have proved effective, although it must be applied with care, for used too strong, it may cause discoloration. Liquid derris is safer, although aerosols or smokes of malathion or gamma, and B.H.C. have proved most effective.

Where attacks are known to have occurred, it is helpful if the stools of those being used for cuttings are given a few sprays of a weak solution of Sybol insecticide, and the rooted cuttings, too, should be given a spraying.

STOOL MINER

Less common than the Leaf Miner, there is another pest known as *Psila nigricornis*, of which the maggots burrow into the rootstock and bases of the stem. In bad cases, new growths from which cuttings can be taken are slow to form and no suitable material at all may develop. From the little at present known of this pest, it does seem that Gamma, B.H.C., or Dieldrin sprays give a fair control. Fortunately, this is not a trouble which is very likely to appear on healthy stocks.

CHRYSANTHEMUM EELWORM

This pest has the ungainly but perhaps appropriate name of *Aphelenchoides ritzema-bosi* and is serious and most troublesome in many seasons.

The first signs of attack are usually seen in the lower leaves, which have yellow or bronze-purple blotches on them. As these blotches increase in size, they become almost black and the dying leaves shrivel and usually fall to the ground.

Eelworms are very tiny and usually travel up the stems and then on to the lateral growth in a film of water. They actually enter the leaves through the minute breathing pores. The pest is spread on stools and cuttings, often, of course, without there being any signs of its presence at propagating time.

Once it is known that eelworm have been present, fresh, clean stocks should never be grown in the same ground, unless the soil has been sterilised. Such new stocks are liable to become blind and stunted if they are planted in infested soil. Eelworms seem able to overwinter in the green tissues of the stools, so that when cuttings are taken they contain the pests.

Although experiments on the control of eelworm are still in progress and various 'dips' are being used, the standard preventive which has proved effective over quite a long period, is the warm water treatment. This is done during the dormant period. The stools are washed free of soil and are placed in a bath of water kept at a temperature of 115 degrees F. for five minutes or, 110 degrees F. for twenty to thirty minutes. There is less possibility of any damage to the more sensitive varieties with the five minute treatment. As soon as treated the stools should be washed in clean cold water and planted at once in clean soil. Occasionally new growths for cuttings are slower in developing after the treatment has been carried out, but the check can be lessened by keeping the stools in a temperature of around 50 degrees F. and being careful with the watering.

A good measure of control of eelworm can also be obtained by using a spray of parathion once the cuttings have rooted with a second application after four or five weeks. This is a very poisonous preparation, however, and should always be used with the utmost care. One simple way of reducing the possibility of eelworm is to avoid growing chrysanthemums on the same ground year after year.

A method of preventing the eelworm from ascending higher up the plant is to smear the main stem with a band of vaseline. Old and dead leaves and stems should always be removed and burned

MISCELLANEOUS PESTS

Apart from the more serious enemies already dealt with, there are a number of others which occasionally do minor damage.

Slugs will sometimes attack the young shoots when they are developing into the cutting stage. When the plants have been in the open ground during the summer and are lifted in the autumn it sometimes happens that slug eggs are in the soil around the base of the plants. This is one reason why some growers wash off the soil from the roots of the plants before taking them to the greenhouse or frame. Slugs can usually be destroyed by using one of the proprietary slug baits having a base of metaldehyde, either in dust or liquid form.

Woodlice will often eat into the young growths when stools are in the greenhouse or frames. A dusting of D.D.T. powder usually clears them, especially if it is also applied to any near-by crevices where the pests may hide and breed. Leather Jackets also spoil the young shoots and may even sever them from the stool, while they will occasionally attack older, harder stems. Apart from traps of portions of potatoes, carrots, etc., from which the pests can be destroyed, B.H.C. or aldrin dust controls Leather Jackets.

Earwigs sometimes damage the flowers. They can be caught by putting hay or straw in inverted flower pots on canes, or in the greenhouse they can be 'smoked' out.

Wireworms attack both roots and stems and can cause the death of a plant. There are several wireworm killers in powder form which can be worked into the soil or dusted on the surface around the plants.

Another minor but very real nuisance is sometimes caused by birds soon after plants have been put out in May and June. Young plants may have their leaves stripped off for no known reason. Apart from the more obvious ways of keeping birds away, the old fashioned method of stretching strands of black cotton over the plants is very effective in stopping the attacks.

Index

Anemone-centred Varieties, 98–99
Annuals for Cutting, 54, 167–71
Aphids, 181
Artificial Fertilisers, 55–56
Autumn Sowing, 170

Bagging Blooms, 77–79
Basal Cuttings, 30, 34
Bird Damage, 187
Blanchard, Louis Pierre, 13
Bone Meal, 20
Bordeaux Mixture, 173
Botrytis, 175–6
Boxes, 50–54
Brush Chrysanthemums, 158
Bregnius, 12
Bunching Blooms, 51–53

Canes, 69
Capsid Bugs, 183–4
Cascade Chrysanthemums, 107–10
Charcoal, 26
Charm Chrysanthemums, 110–11
Chinese species, 15
Chromosomes, 155
Chrysanthemum Arrangements, 142
Cold Frames, 119
Composts, 23–26
Crocking Pots, 43, 46
Cutting Blooms, 50

Delaux, Simon, 13
Derris, 185
Diseases, 172–9
Dividing Plants, 73
Disbudding, 95

Early Varieties, 65–79
Edible Chrysanthemums, 160–1
Eelworms, 28, 188–9
Estimating, 37
Exhibiting Blooms, 95
Exhibition Varieties, 102–4, 132–42

Fish Guano, 20
Flower Scorch, 174
Feeding, 47, 54, 59, 95
Filling Pots, 43
Firm Potting, 43, 47
Foliar Feeding, 58–59
Fortune, Robert, 13
Fungicide, 173
Fumigating, 100–1
Frost, 44

Grading, 51–52
Greaseproof Bags, 72

Harvest Giants, 158
Heat Therapy, 178–9
Hoof and Horn, 20
Hormone Powder, 33
Heated Frames, 33
House Decoration, 148–50
Housing Plants, 121

Insecticides, 77, 181–2
Interplanting, 89

Jamaica Primrose, 11
Japanese Varieties, 102–4
John Innes Compost, 23–26, 43, 55, 74
Judging Blooms, 139–42

Korean Varieties, *86–87*

Late Struck Cuttings, *35*
Late Varieties, *100–6*
Leaf Miner, *184–5*
Leaf Scorch, *66*
Lilliputs, *156*
Lifting Plants, *112, 117, 162*
Lime, *18, 21*
Liquid Feeding, *22*
Loam, *24–25*
Long Day Treatment, *143–7*

Manures, 26
Marketing, *50–54*
Mid-Season Varieties, *104–6*
Miniature Anemone-flowered, *159*

National Chrysanthemum Society, *11, 13–14*
New Fantasy Variety, *159*

Organic Fertilisers, *55, 65*
Organic Matter, *17–19*
Otley Koreans, *88*

Packing, *50–54*
Perpetual flowering, *157*
Pests, *180–7*
Pollination, *152*
Polythene, *72*
Pompon varieties, *80–85*
Potash, *21*
Pot Culture, *118–22*
Potting, *42, 45, 75, 119*
Propagation by Cuttings, *27–37*
    by Division, *40*
    from Seed, *38–41*

Rayonnante Varieties, *41, 148, 159*
Raising New Varieties, *151–5*
Red Spider, *184*
Ring Culture, *60–64*
Rubellum Varieties, *91–93*
Russian Species, *15*

Salter, John, *13*
Seaweed Manure, *57*
Seed Sowing, *153*
Scented Chrysanthemums, *161*
Shasta Daisy, *19, 163*
Shoddy, *57*
Short Day Treatment, *143–7*
Soil requirements, *17–26*
Silver Sand, *26*
Sites, *17–18*
Size of Plants, *27*
Single Varieties, *94–99*
Species, *11–12, 14–16, 86, 91, 163, 169–70*
Sports, *153–4*
Spoon Chrysanthemums, *159*
Spider Chrysanthemums, *160*
Spray Varieties, *80–85*
Staking Plants, *48*
Stools, *28–30, 36*
Stem Cuttings, *34*
Stopping Plants, *120, 123, 131*
Supporting Plants, *37*
Summer Propagation, *36*

Temperatures, *33*
Timing Flowers, *123–31, 145–7*
Tip Cuttings, *179*
Top Dressing, *19, 95–96*

Unheated Greenhouses, *44*

Vases and Containers, *149*
Ventilation, *45*
Vernalisation, *30*
Vermiculite, *31–32*
Virus Diseases, *178–9, 181*

Weldmesh Supports, *70*
Warm Water Treatment, *34*
Wild Species, *12*
Wilt, *174*
White Fly, *183–4*
Woody Shoots, *30*

Year Round Production, *143–7*